THE
MISSION

JOINING GOD IN HIS WORK

LifeWay Press®
Nashville, Tennessee

+‡+DISCIPLES PATH

Disciples Path is a series of studies founded on Jesus' model of discipleship. Created by experienced disciple makers across the nation, it offers an intentional pathway for transformational discipleship and a way to help followers of Christ move from new disciples to mature disciple makers. Each study in the series is built on the principles of modeling, practicing, and multiplying:

- Leaders model the life of a biblical disciple.

- Disciples follow and practice from the leader.

- Disciples become disciple makers and multiply through the *Disciples Path*.

Each study in the series has been written and approved by disciple makers for small groups and one-on-one settings.

Contributors:

Dr. Rod Dempsey; Thomas Road Baptist Church; Lynchburg, Virginia

Chuan Anderson; First Baptist Church; Palm Coast, Florida

MINISTRY GRID
training made simple

For helps on how to use *Disciples Path,* tips on how to better lead groups, or additional ideas for leading this study, visit ministrygrid.com/web/disciplespath.

© 2015 LifeWay Press® • Reprinted October 2020

ISBN 978-1-4300-4032-3 • Item 005727822

Dewey decimal classification: 266
Subject heading: EVANGELISTIC WORK \ MISSIONS \ DISCIPLESHIP

Eric Geiger
Vice President, LifeWay Resources

Sam O'Neal, Joel Polk
Content Editors

Brian Daniel
Manager, Short-Term Discipleship

Michael Kelley
Director, Groups Ministry

We believe that the Bible has God for its author; salvation for its end; and truth, without any mixture of error, for its matter and that all Scripture is totally true and trustworthy. To review LifeWay's doctrinal guideline, visit lifeway.com/doctrinalguideline.

Unless indicated otherwise, Scripture quotations are taken from the Holman Christian Standard Bible®, copyright 1999, 2000, 2002, 2003, 2009 by Holman Bible Publishers. Used by permission. Scripture quotations marked NIV are taken from the Holy Bible, NEW INTERNATIONAL VERSION®. Copyright © 1973, 1978, 1984 by Biblica Inc. All rights reserved worldwide. Used by permission.

To order additional copies of this resource, write to LifeWay Resources Customer Service; One LifeWay Plaza; Nashville, TN 37234; fax 615-251-5933; call toll free 800-458-2772; or order online at LifeWay.com; email orderentry@lifeway.com.

Printed in the United States of America

Groups Ministry Publishing • LifeWay Resources
One LifeWay Plaza • Nashville, TN 37234

CONTENTS

A NOTE FOR DISCIPLE MAKERS

Several years ago I was part of a massive research study that sought to discover how the Lord often brings about transformation in the hearts of His people. The study became a book called *Transformational Discipleship*. Basically, we wanted to learn how disciples are made. Based on the study of Scripture and lots of interactions with people, we concluded that transformation is likely to occur when a godly **leader** applies **truth** to the heart of a person while that person is in a teachable **posture.**

- **LEADER:** You are the leader. As you invest in the people you're discipling, they will learn much about the Christian faith by watching you, by sensing your heart for the Lord, and by seeing you pursue Him. I encourage you to seek to be the type of leader who can say, "Follow my example as I follow the example of Christ."

- **TRUTH:** All six studies in the *Disciples Path* series were developed in deep collaboration with ministry leaders who regularly and effectively disciple people. The studies are designed to take the people you disciple into the Word of God—because we're confident that Jesus and His Word sanctify us and transform us. Our community of disciple makers mapped out a path of the truths we believe are essential for each believer to know and understand.

- **POSTURE:** Hopefully the people you will be investing in adopt a teachable posture—one that is open and hungry for the Lord. Encourage them to take the study seriously and to view your invitation to study together as a sacred opportunity to experience the grace of God and the truth of God.

We hope and pray the Lord will use this study in your life and the lives of those you disciple. As you apply the truth of God to teachable hearts, transformation will occur. Thank you for being a disciple maker!

In Christ,

Eric

Eric Geiger
Vice President at LifeWay Christian Resources
Coauthor of *Transformational Discipleship*

WHAT IS A DISCIPLE?

Congratulations! If you've chosen to live as a disciple of Jesus, you've made the most important decision imaginable. But you may be wondering, *What does it mean to be a disciple?*

To put it simply, a disciple of Jesus is someone who has chosen to follow Jesus. That's the command Jesus gave to those He recruited as His first disciples: "Follow Me." In Jesus' culture, religious leaders called rabbis would gather a group of followers called disciples to follow in their footsteps and learn their teachings. In the same way, you will become more and more like Jesus as you purposefully follow Him in the weeks to come. Jesus once said, "Everyone who is fully trained will be like his teacher" (Luke 6:40).

On a deeper level, disciples of Jesus are those learning to base their identities on Jesus Himself. All of us use different labels to describe who we are at the core levels of our hearts. Some think of themselves as athletes or intellectuals. Others think of themselves as professionals, parents, leaders, class clowns, and so on.

Disciples of Jesus set aside those labels and base their identities on Him. For example:

- **A disciple of Jesus is a child of God.** In the Bible we find these words: "Look at how great a love the Father has given us that we should be called God's children. And we are!" (1 John 3:1). We are God's children. He loves us as our perfect Father.

- **A disciple of Jesus is an alien in this world.** Disciples of Jesus are aliens, or outsiders, in their own cultures. Because of this identity, Jesus' disciples abstain from actions and activities that are contrary to Him. Peter, one of Jesus' original disciples, wrote these words: "Dear friends, I urge you as strangers and temporary residents to abstain from fleshly desires that war against you" (1 Pet. 2:11).

- **A disciple of Jesus is an ambassador for Christ.** Another of Jesus' disciples recorded these words in the Bible: "Therefore, if anyone is in Christ, he is a new creation; old things have passed away, and look, new things have come. Therefore, we are ambassadors for Christ, certain that God is appealing through us. We plead on Christ's behalf, 'Be reconciled to God'" (2 Cor. 5:17,20). Ambassadors represent their king and country in a different culture for a specified period of time. Because we have been transformed by Jesus and are now His disciples and ambassadors, we represent Him to the world through our actions and by telling others about Him.

The journey you are about to take is one that will transform you more and more to be like Jesus. Enjoy! No one ever loved and cared for people more passionately than Jesus. No one was ever more sincere in His concern for others than Jesus. And no one ever gave more so that we could experience His love than Jesus did on the cross.

As you grow to be more like Jesus, you'll find that your relationships are stronger, you have more inner peace than ever before, and you look forward to the future as never before.

That's the blessing of living as a disciple of Jesus.

HOW TO USE THIS RESOURCE

Welcome to *The Mission*. By exploring the journey of Jesus' earliest disciples, both new and established Christians will gain a better understanding of what it means to follow Christ. As you get started, consider the following guides and suggestions for making the most of this experience.

GROUP DISCUSSION

Because the process of discipleship always involves at least two people—the leader and the disciple—each session of *The Mission* includes a practical plan for group engagement and discussion.

This plan includes the following steps:

- **GET STARTED.** The first section of the group material helps you ease into the discussion by starting on common ground. You'll begin by reflecting on the previous session and your recent experiences as a disciple. After spending time in prayer, you'll find a practical illustration to help you launch into the main topic of the current session.

- **THE STORY.** While using *Disciples Path*, you'll find opportunities to engage the Bible through both story and teaching. That's why the group time for each session features two main sections: **Know the Story** and **Unpack the Story. Know the Story** introduces a biblical text and includes follow-up questions for brief discussion. It's recommended that your group encounter the biblical text by reading it out loud. **Unpack the Story** includes practical teaching material and discussion questions—both designed to help you engage the truths contained in the biblical text. To make the most of your experience, use the provided material as a launching point for deeper conversation. As you read through the teaching material and engage the questions as a group, be thinking of how the truths you're exploring will impact your everyday life.

- **ENGAGE.** The group portion of each session ends with an activity designed to help you practice the biblical principles introduced in **Know the Story** and more fully explored in **Unpack the Story.** This part of the group time often appeals to different learning styles and will push you to engage the text at a personal level.

INDIVIDUAL DISCOVERY

Each session of *The Mission* also includes content for individual use during the time between group gatherings. This content is divided into three categories:

⬆ **Worship:** features content for worship and devotion. These activities provide opportunities for you to connect with God in meaningful ways and deepen your relationship with Him.

➡ ⬅ **Personal study:** features content for personal study. These pages help you gain a deeper understanding of the truths and principles explored during the group discussion.

⬅ ➡ **Application:** features content for practical application. These suggestions help you take action based on the information you've learned and your encounters with God.

Note: Aside from the **Reading Plan,** the content provided in the Individual Discovery portion of each session should be considered optional. You'll get the most out of your personal study by working with your group leader to create a personalized discipleship plan using the **Weekly Activities** checklist included in each session.

ADDITIONAL SUGGESTIONS

- You'll be best prepared for each group discussion or mentoring conversation if you read the session material beforehand. A serious read will serve you most effectively, but skimming the **Get Started** and **The Story** sections will also be helpful if time is limited.

- The deeper you're willing to engage in the group discussions and individual discovery each session, the more you'll benefit from those experiences. Don't hold back, and don't be afraid to ask questions whenever necessary.

- As you explore the **Engage** portion of each session, you'll have the chance to practice different activities and spiritual disciplines. Take advantage of the chance to observe others during the group time—and to ask questions—so that you'll be prepared to incorporate these activities into your private spiritual life as well.

- Visit lifeway.com/disciplespath for a free PDF download that includes leader helps for *The Mission* and additional resources for disciple makers.

CHRIST CAME TO US

We are His mission; He is our solution.

REFLECT

Welcome to *The Mission*. This resource will help you gain a deeper understanding of your mission as a follower of Jesus who lives, works, and plays in a world that's often opposed to Him. Not surprisingly, your study will begin with Jesus Himself.

The first half of this study will explore Christ's incarnation in the world, His mission for the world, and His death to save the world. The second half will outline our responsibilities as disciples: We're called to die with Christ, to go with Christ as individuals, and to go with Christ as a community to advance His kingdom in our world. That's our mission.

Use the following questions to begin this session with discussion.

How would you describe your goals as a disciple of Jesus?

What do you hope to learn or experience in the weeks to come?

PRAY

Stop for a moment to pray, either individually or as a group:

- Thank God for your own salvation and for the salvation of your friends and family who have joined you in following Christ.

- Ask Him to fill you afresh with awe and wonder over His gift of salvation.

- Ask God to provide meaningful connections between you and those in your path who have yet to commit their lives to Him.

INTRODUCTION

"Here I come to save the day!"

Do you remember the old *Mighty Mouse* cartoons? The main character was an animated, anthropomorphic mouse in a suit and cape. He had a wide range of powers—flight, super strength, X-ray vision, telekinesis, and more—all of which he used to free victim after victim from the clutches of evil foes.

Each time Mighty Mouse achieved victory over his adversary, an unseen audience would erupt in loud applause as orchestral music played in the background. Then the narrator would say, "What a mouse. *What* a mouse!"

Who were some of your favorite heroes growing up?

What powers or characteristics in these heroes did you appreciate most?

Most people enjoy hero stories. Whether real or imagined, we appreciate the thought of someone powerful coming to the rescue of those in need. We're also grateful for the compassion, or even the sense of duty, that would compel one person to help another.

Perhaps what we like best about hero stories, however, is the way rescue always seems to occur just in the nick of time. Can you picture that moment in your mind? The situation is grim. The forces of evil are on the cusp of accomplishing their goals, and the very lives of innocent people are about to be thrown away.

Then, right at the moment when the last of our hope slips away, we hear it: "Here I come to save the day!" Salvation has come.

This session is a reminder that all of us who have trusted in Christ have experienced that moment. When humanity was hopelessly snared in sin—when we had no hope of pulling ourselves away from the forces of evil inside our own hearts—God sent His Son to meet our most pressing need.

Christ came to us with a mission, and He has won the day.

KNOW THE STORY

In today's culture we're often tempted to think of the Christmas story as a self-contained event. We celebrate the birth of Jesus, but we don't always remember that He was born with a purpose. Christ came on a mission to save us from our sin.

18 The birth of Jesus Christ came about this way: After His mother Mary had been engaged to Joseph, it was discovered before they came together that she was pregnant by the Holy Spirit. 19 So her husband Joseph, being a righteous man, and not wanting to disgrace her publicly, decided to divorce her secretly.

20 But after he had considered these things, an angel of the Lord suddenly appeared to him in a dream, saying, "Joseph, son of David, don't be afraid to take Mary as your wife, because what has been conceived in her is by the Holy Spirit. 21 She will give birth to a son, and you are to name Him Jesus, because He will save His people from their sins."

22 Now all this took place to fulfill what was spoken by the Lord through the prophet:

> 23 See, the virgin will become pregnant
> and give birth to a son,
> and they will name Him Immanuel,

which is translated "God is with us."

24 When Joseph got up from sleeping, he did as the Lord's angel had commanded him. He married her 25 but did not know her intimately until she gave birth to a son. And he named Him Jesus.
MATTHEW 1:18-25

What thoughts or memories come to mind when you read these verses? Why?

UNPACK THE STORY

SALVATION COMES THROUGH A PERSON

We can't properly appreciate the concept of salvation until we think deeply about the Person of Jesus Christ. Why? Because Jesus is more than the One who accomplished our salvation; He's not simply the Being who made salvation possible.

Instead, Jesus *is* our salvation.

When you embraced the call to follow Christ, you didn't respond to a concept or a message. You responded to a Person. You followed Jesus—the same Jesus who was born of a virgin, grew, learned, lived, and died almost 2,000 years ago. The same Jesus who is Lord of God's kingdom and Master of your life.

When you consider your coworkers, friends, and family members who have not yet experienced salvation, you want that to change. You want them to experience the joy that comes with the forgiveness of sin—and that's good. That's natural. But they won't experience that joy by better understanding a doctrine or by reciting a prayer.

They need to meet Jesus. They need to experience Him.

When you embraced the call to follow Christ, you didn't respond to a concept or a message. You responded to a Person.

What do you remember about the first time you encountered Jesus in a personal way?

When was the last time you enjoyed a personal encounter with Jesus?

The Gospel writers understood the importance of Jesus' existence as a living, breathing Person. That's why Matthew made a point of starting his record of Jesus' life by writing about His miraculous birth. Luke did the same. And John opened his Gospel with a similar truth expressed in a more abstract form: "The Word became flesh and took up residence among us" (John 1:14).

How does Jesus' Personhood help you follow Him?

SALVATION COMES WITH A PLAN

The message of the gospel is simple: By sending Jesus to us, God made a way where there was no way. God has a plan of rescue for all humanity. God's plan is not just a good plan, or even the best of many plans—it's the *only* plan sufficient to meet the most pressing need in our lives: the need to be rescued from our sin.

We've seen that salvation is anchored in the Person of Jesus Christ. But simply knowing who Jesus is and what He's done isn't enough to actually accomplish the forgiveness of our sins. God's plan involves each person encountering Jesus in a way that leads to a relationship with Him.

And still there's more. Once we encounter Jesus, we must respond to Him with faith, which is an act of the will in which we place our trust in Him.

What are some common misconceptions about salvation?

To think about salvation in another way, God's plan requires that all people:

- **Realize:** The first step in being rescued is to realize we're in trouble. God's plan is for everyone to realize that they're not sufficient to save themselves—that Jesus is the only way of rescue from the corruption of sin.

- **Repent:** Once we realize our situation, we must repent. To repent involves being genuinely sorry for sin. It means changing our minds about our behavior and actively turning away from sin and toward God.

- **Receive:** Salvation comes as an offer—a gift—of God's grace. And that gift must be accepted as an act of faith.

These concepts may seem basic, but it's vital to have a firm foundation as we continue to explore our mission as disciples of Jesus.

> Once we encounter Jesus, we must respond to Him with faith, which is an act of the will in which we place our trust in Him.

How can we help others recognize and follow these steps?

ENGAGE

To live as a disciple of Jesus means joining Him in accomplishing His mission for the world. As we'll see throughout this study, we have a part to play in helping others recognize the reality of their sin and turn to Jesus for salvation. Sometimes that part includes directly sharing the gospel message. Other times our contributions are more subtle.

For example, prayer is one of the most important things we can do for those who have yet to experience salvation in Christ.

Make a list of at least five people in your spheres of influence who are not yet disciples of Jesus. Commit to praying daily for each of these people by name. Ask God to send His Spirit and convict them of their sin.

1.

2.

3.

4.

5.

PRAYER REQUESTS

....

....

....

....

....

....

....

....

In addition to studying God's Word, work with your group leader to create a plan for personal study, worship, and application between now and the next session. Select from the following optional activities to match your personal preferences and available time.

↑ Worship

☑ Read your Bible. Complete the reading plan on page 16.

☐ Connect with God each day through prayer.

☐ Spend time with God by engaging the devotional experience on page 17.

➡ ⬅ Personal Study

☐ Read and interact with "Identifying with Jesus" on page 18.

☐ Read and interact with "Preparing to Be a Witness" on page 20.

⬅ ➡ Application

☐ Make an effort to deepen your relationship with an acquaintance this week. Seek out someone you'd like to know better and start a conversation.

☐ Memorize Luke 19:10: "The Son of Man has come to seek and to save the lost."

☐ Continue praying daily for the people in your life who need to experience salvation. Seek opportunities to speak with these people in meaningful ways—and especially keep an eye open for chances to share the gospel message.

☐ Dig deeper into the doctrine of salvation by listening to a podcast on that subject from a respected teacher. You could also read a book, listen to a sermon, or study an article.

☐ Other:

 **WORSHIP**

READING PLAN

By describing the earliest days of the church, the Book of Acts offers helpful information and inspiration for joining God in His mission. Use the space provided to record your thoughts and responses as you read.

Day 1
Acts 1:1-14

Day 2
Acts 1:15-26

Day 3
Acts 2:1-36

Day 4
Acts 2:37-47

Day 5
Acts 3:1-26

Day 6
Acts 4:1-22

Day 7
Acts 4:23-37

THE WORD

The central truth of this resource is that God came to earth with a mission to redeem His people through the forgiveness of their sins and that He has called His followers—those who've already experienced forgiveness—to participate in that mission. This is the gospel, the good news.

As you contemplate the gospel and prepare to engage in the mission of sharing that truth with others, remember that everything begins and ends with Jesus. He is the embodiment of the gospel. He is the Word made flesh, as the apostle John reminded us:

> The Word became flesh
> and took up residence among us.
> We observed His glory,
> the glory as the One and Only Son from the Father,
> full of grace and truth.
> **JOHN 1:14**

Jesus is God and was God from "the beginning" (John 1:1). He is God the Son, the second Person of the Trinity. Remaining God, not becoming anything less than fully God or anything other than God, Jesus took on human flesh. Why did He do this? Because all flesh was corrupt. Only a complete and perfect sacrifice could satisfy forever God's righteous requirement for justice against sin (see Rom. 3:25).

At the same time, Jesus exists as a man. He came into the world as a baby, born of a virgin (see Matt. 1:18-25; Luke 1:26-38). Jesus lived a span of decades as a person and experienced life as we do. Fully identifying Himself with us, He experienced the normal process of growth and development. He encountered the full breadth of human experiences: heat and cold, hunger and thirst, work and rest.

Jesus had to be made like us in all things in order to qualify as the substitute for our sins—and to help us when we're tested (see Heb. 2:17-18). He was one with us in every way, except that He did not sin. Jesus lived a perfect life and offered Himself as a sacrifice in order to save us from our sins.

What have you learned about Jesus through your own experiences?

How would you like to experience Jesus in the days and years to come?

➡ ⬅ PERSONAL STUDY

IDENTIFYING WITH JESUS

Here's a truth that's worth repeating: Jesus didn't come to earth simply to secure our salvation; He *is* our salvation. His mission involved making Himself available to all people as the solution to our primary problem. He came so that we could believe in Him and therefore receive forgiveness from our sin.

As we saw in Matthew 1:18-25, the way Jesus came into our world was totally unique in the scope of history. While any other king would have been born in a palace, Jesus was born in a stable. While any other king's coming would have been heralded throughout the kingdom and widely publicized to all available subjects, the announcement of Jesus' birth was given only to a few humble witnesses (see Matt. 1:20-23; Luke 1:26-35; Luke 2:9-14). While other children are given names that shape who they will become, the name given to Jesus declared who He already was.

Given the uniqueness of Jesus' incarnation, it's no surprise that people reacted in a number of different ways to His presence in the world.

> *Read the following passages of Scripture and record the different ways people responded to Jesus.*
>
> *Matthew 2:1-12*
>
>
> *Matthew 2:13-18*
>
>
> *Luke 2:8-20*
>
>
> *Luke 2:36-38*
>
>
> *Luke 4:16-30*

As disciples of Jesus, we are called to participate in His mission to redeem the world. We have experienced Christ as our salvation, and therefore we work to help others experience Him as well. Yet, we must understand that joining Jesus in His mission means we will encounter a number of different reactions and responses, as He did.

There will be times when people respond to your work with joy. They will see your actions and hear as you proclaim the gospel, and they will be glad. They will welcome you into their lives even as they welcome Christ into their hearts.

There will be other times, however, when people respond to your work in negative ways, including bitterness, scorn, anger, and even rage. When you join Jesus in His mission to redeem the world, you will experience strife and strain in your relationships, both personal and public. You will experience persecution in different forms. You will be confused at times, frustrated and angry at other times.

And Jesus knew all of this when He called you to follow Him:

> 18 If the world hates you, understand that it hated Me before it hated you. 19 If you were of the world, the world would love you as its own. However, because you are not of the world, but I have chosen you out of it, the world hates you. 20 Remember the word I spoke to you: "A slave is not greater than his master." If they persecuted Me, they will also persecute you. If they kept My word, they will also keep yours.
> **JOHN 15:18-20**

When have you experienced negative interactions or negative emotions in your efforts to follow Jesus?

What rewards have you experienced while participating in Jesus' mission for the world?

Jesus encountered trouble as He worked to redeem the people of this world. We will encounter the same. Yet, by following His example—by modeling His courage and reflecting His resolve—we can continue to persevere as disciples of Christ on a mission in our world.

PERSONAL STUDY

PREPARING TO BE A WITNESS

The Bible teaches that there is no hope for anyone who doesn't believe and receive God's plan of salvation by accepting Jesus Christ. Think deeply about that for a moment. In the world today there are really only two groups of people: those who are saved and those who are lost. Yet, the wonderful news of the gospel is that Jesus came to save us all. Through a step of faith, the fate of lost people can be changed forever.

Those of us who have been rescued and reconciled to God have been entrusted with the message of salvation (see Matt. 28:18-20) and the ministry of reconciling others to Him (see 2 Cor. 5:18-20). How do we do that? Where should we start? How do we ready ourselves to be instruments for reconciling others to God?

Here are a few ideas to begin preparing yourself for life as a witness to God's plan of salvation.

1. Memorize and meditate on the Scriptures. Apart from knowing the Savior ourselves, there is little else that helps our confidence as witnesses more than knowing God's Word. Memorize a few verses and passages that explain what salvation is and why we need it. This discipline helps us be ready to share the truth whenever or wherever an opportunity presents itself.

If you're new to Bible memorization, the following Scripture passages are a great place to start:

- Romans 3:23-24
- Romans 5:8
- Romans 6:23
- Romans 10:9-10

What Bible verses will you memorize in the coming weeks?

2. Move toward unsaved people. Jesus came to seek and save the lost, which means He sought to encounter them. He looked for ways to engage with them. Likewise, we should look for opportunities to develop relationships with unsaved people. Grocery store clerks, neighbors, homeless people, barbers, coworkers, coaches—all who are not yet following Christ—these make up our mission field. Consider ways you can get to know these individuals in your sphere of influence in order to impact their spiritual condition.

As you identify people who need to experience Jesus as their salvation, be proactive in deepening those relationships. Pursue them with love, friendship, and patience. Knowing the lost people in your community will help you understand how to share with them in a way that intersects with their lives.

Which people in your life need to experience salvation? Make a list.

3. Make prayer for lost people a priority. When we pray for those who need salvation, we stand as intercessors between God and them, seeking to bring God closer to them and them closer to God. As we plead for God's intervention in the lives of lost people, He begins to work in their hearts. Not only that, He also begins to sensitize our hearts to the point where we share His burden for them.

No one wants the lost to be saved more than God. By seeking Him, He also opens our eyes to opportunities to share with them.

Commit to praying each day for the people on your list (above).

4. Prepare your personal testimony. The story of what Christ has done for you personally is one of the greatest tools you have for leading others to an awareness of the Lord's calling on their lives. When people see and hear you, they encounter living proof of the power of Christ to save a soul and transform a life.

It's important that you're able to share your testimony in a concise, straight-to-the-point manner. Perhaps the simplest way to be sure that what you share is clear and concise is to write it out. Doing so helps make a long story short. And committing your testimony to memory helps you be able to share it whenever or wherever an opportunity arises.

How would you describe your testimony? See if you can record it in the space below.

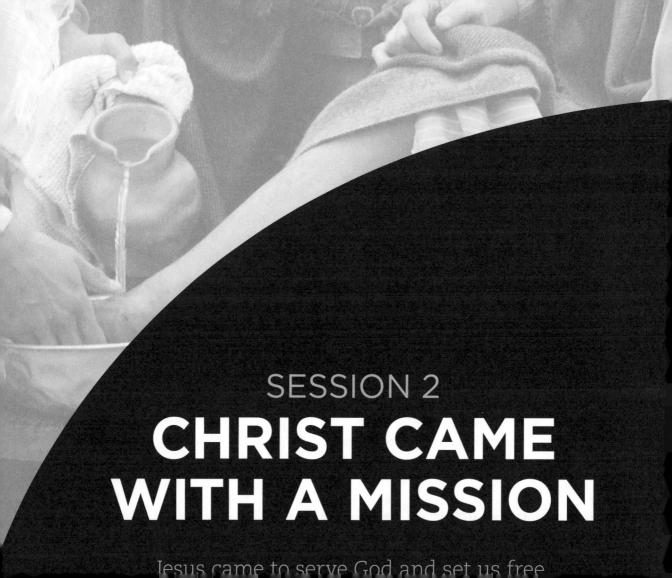

SESSION 2

CHRIST CAME
WITH A MISSION

Jesus came to serve God and set us free.

REFLECT

In the previous session we focused on Jesus' presence in this world. We know from God's Word that Jesus left heaven and entered our world in a physical way—an event we often refer to as the incarnation. We also reinforced the truth that Jesus is our only hope for salvation. He is the only solution to the problem of our sin.

As you prepare to dig deeper into the mission at the core of Jesus' incarnation, take a moment to reflect on your experiences in recent days.

Which of the assignments did you explore this week? How did it go?

What did you learn or experience while reading the Bible?

What questions would you like to ask?

PRAY

Stop for a moment to pray, either individually or as a group:

- Thank God for actively engaging in His mission to redeem the world.

- Ask Him to come alongside those who are not saved and to help them become free from their sin and spiritual blindness.

- Ask for wisdom and clarity of mind as you study God's Word in your group and throughout the coming week.

INTRODUCTION

The Secret Millionaire is a reality TV series in which super-wealthy individuals live undercover for a week in an impoverished or deprived community. The millionaires willingly volunteer to leave their homes, conceal their identities, and deny themselves the privileges of fortune in order to live in poverty.

Having physically relocated to a neighborhood in need, the millionaires share the living conditions of their new neighbors by taking residence in a local housing project and cutting themselves back to welfare-level wages. They intentionally connect with the community by living among the people and identifying with their experiences. Their nearness allows them to observe real life and real situations. It also provides opportunities to connect with their neighbors' struggles, share in their distresses, and grieve their lack of basic necessities.

Watching and listening, the millionaires consider what could be done to relieve the suffering around them and improve the lives of their new neighbors. On the last day before returning to paradise, the millionaires reveal their true identities and surprise a person or group of people with a generous endowment from their own fortunes.

How would you describe the way you feel when you're able to help someone?

What are some of the more significant needs in your church congregation? Your community?

The Secret Millionaire offers a great example of how an empathetic presence, generous provisions, and empowered people can help make tough circumstances better. It also offers a helpful reminder of what Jesus did—and is still doing—for all of us.

God sent His one and only Son into the world to bring lasting solutions to the lingering problems of others. He came to both to save and to serve.

KNOW THE STORY

It's often difficult to explain biblical concepts in a short and simple way. That's true today, and it was also true in the early church. That's one of the reasons Christians have treasured the following verses from the Book of Philippians. Known as the "Hymn to Christ," this passage captures both Jesus' identity and His mission in the world:

⁵ Make your own attitude that of Christ Jesus,

> ⁶ who, existing in the form of God,
> did not consider equality with God
> as something to be used for His own advantage.
> ⁷ Instead He emptied Himself
> by assuming the form of a slave,
> taking on the likeness of men.
> And when He had come as a man
> in His external form,
> ⁸ He humbled Himself by becoming obedient
> to the point of death—
> even to death on a cross.
> ⁹ For this reason God highly exalted Him
> and gave Him the name
> that is above every name,
> ¹⁰ so that at the name of Jesus
> every knee will bow—
> of those who are in heaven and on earth
> and under the earth—
> ¹¹ and every tongue should confess
> that Jesus Christ is Lord,
> to the glory of God the Father.
> **PHILIPPIANS 2:5-11**

What's your initial reaction to verse 5?

How do these verses contribute to your understanding of Jesus' mission in our world?

UNPACK THE STORY

CHRIST CAME TO SERVE GOD

There's a common misconception regarding the reasons for Jesus' presence in our world. Specifically, many people believe humanity was the driving force behind the incarnation—that Jesus came to us simply because we needed Him so desperately.

It's certainly true that humanity needed Christ, and still needs Christ. We are hopeless without Him. Yet, it's important to understand that *God* was the primary motivation for Jesus' incarnation. Not us.

In Philippians 2:6-7, Paul reinforced the truth that Jesus is God. The Son has always existed "in the form of God." However, in order to accomplish God's mission to redeem the world, Jesus willingly "emptied Himself" in order to take on the form of man. Specifically, Paul said Jesus became "a slave"—but not to us. Jesus was never a slave or servant of humanity. Rather, Jesus willingly emptied Himself in order to serve God. Verse 8 continues the same idea. By humbling Himself, Jesus was obedient to God's will, not to our needs.

As disciples of Jesus, then, we're called to the same mission and carry the same purpose—to serve God and honor Him.

Why is it dangerous to believe Jesus' mission was based on our needs?

Jesus confirmed His own motivations while speaking to the crowds:

> For I have come down from heaven, not to do My will,
> but the will of Him who sent Me.
> **JOHN 6:38**

Jesus understood that His mission was to serve God and glorify Him. It's great news for us that by doing so, He became our salvation. As disciples of Jesus, then, we're called to the same mission and carry the same purpose—to serve God and honor Him. And, as we'll see throughout this study, one of the ways we serve and honor God is by actively serving as a witness to others.

On a practical level, what does it mean to serve God?

CHRIST CAME TO SET US FREE

Here's another misconception regarding Jesus' mission in our world: that it all began at Christmas. Many people believe that Jesus' birth was the start of God's mission to save humanity from our sins.

Instead, the incarnation was a crucial event in the middle of God's larger plan to set humanity free from the bondage of sin—a plan that stretched all the way back to those first moments after Adam and Eve were exiled from the garden of Eden (see Gen. 3:20-24).

Read the following verses and describe how each one illustrates God's plan to rescue people from their sin.

> *Genesis 12:1-3*
> *Isaiah 53:7-12*
> *Jeremiah 31:31-34*

Jesus is our salvation, which means He is our only hope to experience freedom in a spiritual sense. Jesus' death and resurrection are the only door through which we can pass to receive forgiveness and spiritual life.

Yet, spiritual freedom isn't the only type of freedom Jesus offers those who will follow Him. He can also set us free from our fears and our doubts. He can set us free from emotions that overwhelm us. He can set us free from physical or financial burdens that weigh us down. He can even set us free from the need to control every aspect of our lives and to solve our problems in our own strength—if we let Him.

In short, Jesus can unshackle us from lives focused on temporary struggles and set us free to participate in the glorious unfolding of God's mission for the world.

Jesus' death and resurrection are the only door through which we can pass to receive forgiveness and spiritual life.

In what ways have you experienced freedom in Christ?

Of course, when Jesus sets us free, He also calls us to serve as both witnesses and neighbors to those still stuck in the bondage of their sin.

ENGAGE

When people talk about joining Jesus in His mission for the world, they often use the phrase "sharing the gospel." But what is the *gospel,* specifically? How would you define that term?

In a broad sense, the gospel is everything related to the Person and work of Jesus. This includes everything leading up to His birth, His life, His death, and His resurrection—not to mention all of the benefits believers experience as a result. In a more narrow sense, the gospel refers to the "good news" that all people can be saved from the bondage of their sins through the death and resurrection of Christ.

To "share the gospel" then is simply to talk about that good news. And contrary to the opinions of many, there is no "right" or "correct" way to do so. Just look at the Scriptures!

Read the following passages of Scripture. Compare and contrast each of the different methods used to share the gospel.

Acts 2:14-40

Acts 8:26-35

Acts 17:16-31

PRAYER REQUESTS

....

....

....

....

....

....

....

....

In addition to studying God's Word, work with your group leader to create a plan for personal study, worship, and application between now and the next session. Select from the following optional activities to match your personal preferences and available time.

↑ Worship

☑ Read your Bible. Complete the reading plan on page 30.

☐ Connect with God each day through prayer.

☐ Spend time with God by engaging the devotional experience on page 31.

➡ ⬅ Personal Study

☐ Read and interact with "Christ Calls Us to Serve God" on page 32.

☐ Read and interact with "Christ Calls Us to Serve Others" on page 34.

⬅ ➡ Application

☐ Pray daily for a person or a group of people in your community who need help—spiritual, financial, or otherwise.

☐ Memorize Mark 10:45: "Even the Son of Man did not come to be served, but to serve, and to give His life—a ransom for many."

☐ As part of your devotional life this week, make a special effort to connect with God as your Master and King. Pray, read the Scriptures, and obey God's commands with the mind-set of a servant.

☐ Go out of your way to serve someone this week. Buy coffee for someone who looks cold. Help clean up your coworker's office. Babysit children for a young couple. Do something kind simply to bless someone you know.

☐ Other:

WORSHIP

READING PLAN

Continue exploring the Book of Acts throughout this week. Use the space provided to record your thoughts and responses as you read.

Day 1
Acts 5:1-16

Day 2
Acts 5:17-42

Day 3
Acts 6:1-15

Day 4
Acts 7:1-36

Day 5
Acts 7:37-60

Day 6
Acts 8:1-25

Day 7
Acts 8:26-40

KEEP IT SIMPLE

As human beings, and even as disciples of Jesus, we have a natural tendency to overthink matters that are actually quite simple. Such was the case with the scholar who approached Jesus in Luke 10:

> [25] Just then an expert in the law stood up to test Him, saying, "Teacher, what must I do to inherit eternal life?" [26] "What is written in the law?" He asked him. "How do you read it?"
> [27] He answered:
>> Love the Lord your God with all your heart, with all your soul, with all your strength, and with all your mind; and your neighbor as yourself.
> [28] "You've answered correctly," He told him. "Do this and you will live."
> [29] But wanting to justify himself, he asked Jesus, "And who is my neighbor?"
> **LUKE 10:25-29**

This "expert in the law" was probably a scribe by trade. He may have also served as a Pharisee or teacher of the law. In any event, he approached Jesus with a question that was common among scholars of his day. He wanted to find out Jesus' position on a theological issue in much the same way that a modern politician might ask, "Are you a Democrat or a Republican?"

When Jesus gave his own question back to him, the scholar gave the correct answer. Jesus agreed with him, but that wasn't enough. The scribe wanted to keep going deeper, more complex. He asked, "And who is my neighbor?"

Read Luke 10:30-37 to see Jesus' answer. What strikes you as most interesting about this parable?

Based on this parable, how would you define your neighbors?

Notice the lawyer emphasized who should be the object of love and service, while Jesus emphasized the action itself. Through His parable, Jesus expressed the necessity for less assessment and more action. Moving forward, then, perhaps "Who is my neighbor?" isn't a question we should worry about today. Perhaps we should be asking, "Whose neighbor am I?"

CHRIST CALLS US TO SERVE GOD

When we read through the Scriptures, we find a number of concepts and situations that were common in ancient times but are uncommon today. Think of kings, for example. As modern readers of the Bible, we can recognize the concept of a king on an intellectual level. However, in an era of democracy, it's difficult to really understand what it must have been like to live under the complete, all-powerful rule of a single person.

The same thing is true for the concept of servanthood. As modern readers, we can understand the definition of a *servant* as someone who serves others. However, we typically think of this service in terms of a job. Meaning, the servant serves his or her master for a certain period of time—8 or 10 hours each day, for example—and then "clocks out" to return home and enjoy some rest and relaxation.

In reality, servants in the ancient world were entirely dedicated to meeting the needs and wants of their masters at all times. In fact, it may help us understand things better if we think of the word *slave* instead of *servant*.

> *Read the following passages of Scripture and record what they teach about life as a servant (or slave) in the ancient world.*
>
> *Genesis 16:1-6*
>
>
>
> *Exodus 21:20-21*
>
>
>
> *Deuteronomy 15:12-18*
>
>
>
> *Ephesians 6:5-9*

Why is this important? Because when we accept the call to follow Jesus as His disciples, we are accepting His call to live as servants (or slaves) of God.

As we saw in the group discussion, Jesus Himself came to earth in obedience and service to God. He emptied Himself and assumed "the form of a slave" (Phil. 2:7). As disciples of Jesus, we model Him in all things. Our goal is to become more like Him in every area of life (see 2 Cor. 3:18). Therefore, we follow Christ by joining Him as servants of God.

Sadly, too many Christians believe that serving God is a part-time occupation. When we focus on spiritual things several times throughout our day, we feel justified in pursuing our own interests and desires for the remainder of each day. Again, we often treat serving God as a 9 to 5 occupation, when in reality our identities as disciples of Jesus require a 24/7 commitment.

Jesus Himself made it clear that our service to God must be all-encompassing:

> 7 Which one of you having a slave tending sheep or plowing will say to him when he comes in from the field, "Come at once and sit down to eat"? 8 Instead, will he not tell him, "Prepare something for me to eat, get ready, and serve me while I eat and drink; later you can eat and drink"? 9 Does he thank that slave because he did what was commanded? 10 In the same way, when you have done all that you were commanded, you should say, "We are good-for-nothing slaves; we've only done our duty."
> **LUKE 17:7-10**

What's your initial reaction to these verses? Why?

Do you feel you should be rewarded whenever you obey God by doing something positive or rejecting something negative? Explain.

Jesus has called us to serve God, just as He serves and obeys the Father in all things. The wonderful news is that such service is not a burden or a shackle. Instead, only by fully embracing our identities as servants of God can we experience the fullness of life God designed us to enjoy.

 **PERSONAL STUDY**

CHRIST CALLS US TO SERVE OTHERS

Jesus came to earth with a mission. Though He is God, He willingly emptied Himself in order to enter our world and fulfill that mission, thus serving the Father. As disciples of Jesus, we're also called to serve God, and we're also called to do so by joining Jesus in accomplishing His mission.

Given these truths, it's logical to ask, "What *is* the mission?" What is it we're supposed to aim for or accomplish when we become disciples of Christ? Interestingly, Jesus provided some clear answers to that question when He first announced His ministry (and mission) in a public way:

16 He came to Nazareth, where He had been brought up. As usual, He entered the synagogue on the Sabbath day and stood up to read. 17 The scroll of the prophet Isaiah was given to Him, and unrolling the scroll, He found the place where it was written:

> 18 The Spirit of the Lord is on Me,
> because He has anointed Me
> to preach good news to the poor.
> He has sent Me
> to proclaim freedom to the captives
> and recovery of sight to the blind,
> to set free the oppressed,
> 19 to proclaim the year of the Lord's favor.

20 He then rolled up the scroll, gave it back to the attendant, and sat down. And the eyes of everyone in the synagogue were fixed on Him. 21 He began by saying to them, "Today as you listen, this Scripture has been fulfilled."
LUKE 4:16-21

In what ways did Jesus fulfill the prophecy from Isaiah?

How do these verses help you understand your responsibilities as a disciple of Christ?

Jesus alone could fulfill the spiritual implications of Luke 4:16-21. Through His death and resurrection, He proclaimed good news to those in spiritual poverty, freedom for those held captive to sin, life to those oppressed by the law, and sight to those blind to their own need for salvation.

Still, we can join Jesus in His mission on a practical level. Specifically, we can be:

- **God's messengers.** Jesus shared the good news of the gospel with clarity and variety. He communicated in ways that were mindful of the personalities of individual hearers, relevant to their culture, and sensitive to their needs (see John 3:1-16; 4:3-26; Mark 10:21-22). Likewise, serving God faithfully requires us to be competent, creative, and confident messengers of His salvation. We are called to spread the good news.

- **God's ministers.** Throughout His ministry, Jesus took notice of those who needed help. His mission was primarily spiritual, yet He still took the time to focus on physical needs and earthly troubles. He ministered to the poor, the captives, the blind, and the oppressed—and He has called us to do the same.

- **God's missionaries.** Just as Jesus left paradise in order to save us, we are called to go out of our comfort zones in order to make a difference in the world. This may mean going out into our neighborhoods, going out into our country, or going out across the world. The key is obedience to God's leading and a willingness to go in order to serve those in need.

In what situations do you feel most confident about sharing the gospel?

When you think about people with practical needs, who comes to mind?

Where is God calling you to go in order to serve Him and others?

Jesus met the spiritual and physical needs of those He encountered and those He sought out. As His disciples, we are called to do the same.

CHRIST CAME TO DIE

Jesus came to suffer and to sacrifice—

and to call us to do the same.

REFLECT

In the previous session we took a deeper look at Christ's mission in our world. We saw that He became the salvation for humanity—not in service to humanity, but in service to God. We also learned that Jesus calls us to follow His example by living as servants of God, and that part of our service to God involves intentionally serving other people in order to continue advancing His mission in the world.

As you prepare to engage the climax of Jesus' mission in this world—His death as a sacrifice for the forgiveness of our sin—use the following questions to reflect on your experiences in recent days.

Which of the assignments did you explore this week? How did it go?

What did you learn or experience while reading the Bible?

What questions would you like to ask?

PRAY

Stop for a moment to pray, either individually or as a group:

- Thank God for not withholding any good thing from you, including Jesus.

- Praise God for His plan to make salvation available to all people through the death and resurrection of Jesus.

- Ask God to give you a fresh perspective on suffering and a ready heart to make whatever sacrifices He calls you to make for His glory and for the good of others.

INTRODUCTION

"It was the best of times, it was the worst of times."

The first sentence of Charles Dickens's *A Tale of Two Cities* is one of the most famous opening lines in Western literature, and rightfully so. However, the popularity of that first sentence sometimes overshadows the broader story of the book—a story that is worth remembering because of its striking picture of self-sacrifice for the benefit of others.

Set in London and Paris, the central characters in the book are Charles Darnay and Sydney Carton. Those two men are nearly twins in terms of their physical appearance; yet, they are vastly different on the inside. Darnay is a man of integrity and impeccable character, while Carton is a sly and sarcastic reprobate who drinks too much.

During the story, both men fall in love with Lucie Manette, who represents the ideal woman of her time. Not surprisingly, Lucie chooses to marry Darnay, although Carton becomes a family friend. After years of a peaceful life in London, Darnay is arrested in Paris at the height of the French Revolution because of sins committed by his aristocratic family. He is sentenced to death by guillotine.

At the last moment, however, Carton sneaks into Darnay's prison and knocks him unconscious. Carton arranges to have Darnay smuggled back to London while he remains in prison to ensure his rival's return to Lucie. The next day, Carton is executed in Darnay's place. Carton himself delivers the last line of the book, which is as poignant and powerful as the first: "It is a far, far better thing that I do, than I have ever done; it is a far, far better rest that I go to than I have ever known."[1]

What are some stories from modern culture that reflect the value of self-sacrificial love?

When have you benefited from another person's sacrifice?

Sydney Carton's sacrifice is a moving picture of redemption—a sinful man who willingly died in order to make up for his wasted life. As we'll see in this session, Jesus' sacrifice was something different. In Christ, we see a perfect man who willingly died in order to save the sinful lives of everyone else.

KNOW THE STORY

The truth that Jesus is both fully God and fully human is a foundational doctrine of the Christian faith. And yet it's often hard to imagine Jesus as a genuine human being. It's difficult to think of Jesus, our Lord, encountering such human experiences as loneliness, rejection, and physical pain.

Yet, the Scriptures teach us that Jesus indeed suffered the indignities associated with human life—even the ultimate indignity of physical death.

²⁰ "But you," He asked them, "who do you say that I am?" Peter answered, "God's Messiah!"

²¹ But He strictly warned and instructed them to tell this to no one, ²² saying, "The Son of Man must suffer many things and be rejected by the elders, chief priests, and scribes, be killed, and be raised the third day."

²³ Then He said to them all, "If anyone wants to come with Me, he must deny himself, take up his cross daily, and follow Me. ²⁴ For whoever wants to save his life will lose it, but whoever loses his life because of Me will save it. ²⁵ What is a man benefited if he gains the whole world, yet loses or forfeits himself? ²⁶ For whoever is ashamed of Me and My words, the Son of Man will be ashamed of him when He comes in His glory and that of the Father and the holy angels. ²⁷ I tell you the truth: There are some standing here who will not taste death until they see the kingdom of God."
LUKE 9:20-27

What questions come to mind when you read these verses?

Make a list of the promises contained in these verses.
Which promises strike you as most significant?

UNPACK THE STORY

JESUS SUFFERED

We know from Scripture that Jesus experienced physical suffering on the cross as a necessary part of reconciling humanity with God. Yet, it's also important to recognize the many additional forms of suffering Jesus endured on our behalf:

- **Jesus suffered loneliness.** Jesus was alone in an environment hostile to His way of thinking and contrary to His spiritual composition. He was different from everyone around Him, including His immediate family.

- **Jesus suffered anonymity.** He spent the first 30 years of His life under the radar, unnoticed, uncelebrated, and overlooked by His community (see Mark 6:4). His choice to suffer anonymity can only truly be appreciated when viewed in light of the exaltation He rightly deserved as God.

- **Jesus suffered rejection.** Throughout His public ministry, people threatened Jesus, attempted to bully Him, and even drove Him from their communities. At the end of that ministry, Jesus was abandoned by His closest friends and murdered by the very people He had come to save.

- **Jesus suffered scorn.** Jesus was criticized, accused of demonic activity, slandered, plotted against, interrogated, mocked, spat upon, slapped, wrongfully accused, and beaten to an inch of His life. He was insulted even on the cross as He endured the onset of death. Yet, He did not retaliate against evil people or return their harsh words.

How do you respond to the knowledge that Jesus suffered in these ways and more?

What impact does Jesus' suffering have on your life?

Jesus was never granted a pass from suffering. He endured all the pain and indignity common to human life in our world, not to mention the spiritual torment included with carrying the full weight of our sin. Yet, Jesus demonstrated His power by passing through His suffering in victory—and His example inspires us to strive for the same.

Jesus demonstrated His power by passing through His suffering in victory—and His example inspires us to strive for the same.

JESUS SACRIFICED

The symbol of the cross can mean different things to different people. For some, the cross is an offense—a symbol of a religion they choose to deny. Others see it as a sign of rescue or redemption. Still others as a memorial or symbol of loss.

For any person alive during Jesus' day, the cross was nothing but an instrument of shame, torture, and execution. For Jesus specifically, the cross wasn't just a painful and humiliating responsibility; it was a sentence of ultimate sacrifice—a sentence He willingly chose to carry in unfettered, unflinching obedience to the Father.

Jesus made two foundational choices in His obedience to God. And as you seek to live as Christ's disciple in this world, you must make those choices as well.

First, you must choose to deny yourself. To deny yourself means to give up or surrender all you have and all you are to Jesus. Human management is certain to get in the way of divine ownership. Therefore, living as a disciple of Christ means continually choosing to set aside or even abandon your plans, your interests, your desires, your hopes, and your dreams in order to follow His plans and His interests in the world.

Where do you often experience dissonance between your desires and God's plans?

Second, you must choose to take up your own cross. While the cross was once a symbol of death, it now points to Jesus' faithful execution of God's will. Jesus made a willing sacrifice. As His disciple, you must make the same sacrifice. Having set aside control of your own life, you must take up whatever work Jesus calls you to perform.

Jesus made a willing sacrifice. As His disciple, you must make the same sacrifice.

How would you describe the work Jesus has called you to do?

Disciples of Jesus must deny themselves and take up their crosses. In what ways have you engaged these crucial choices in your own life?

ENGAGE

Many Christians are comfortable with the theory of surrendering to God or submitting to His will. We understand why we should surrender, and we agree that submission is important. But we sometimes forget that genuine submission involves a conscious act. *Surrender* is a verb.

In other words, in order to deny ourselves and take up our crosses, we must actually do something.

Use two or three minutes of private reflection to think about an action or step you can take to intentionally submit yourself to God's will.

As a group, recite Psalm 37:5-9 as a way of affirming your commitment to surrender.

> [5] Commit your way to the LORD;
> trust in Him, and He will act,
> [6] making your righteousness shine like the dawn,
> your justice like the noonday.
>
> [7] Be silent before the LORD and wait expectantly for Him;
> do not be agitated by one who prospers in his way,
> by the man who carries out evil plans.
>
> [8] Refrain from anger and give up your rage;
> do not be agitated—it can only bring harm.
> [9] For evildoers will be destroyed,
> but those who put their hope in the LORD
> will inherit the land.
> **PSALM 37:5-9**

PRAYER REQUESTS

....

....

....

....

1. Charles Dickens, *A Tale of Two Cities* (Mineola, NY: Dover Publications, 1999), 1, 293.

In addition to studying God's Word, work with your group leader to create a plan for personal study, worship, and application between now and the next session. Select from the following optional activities to match your personal preferences and available time.

↑ Worship

☑ Read your Bible. Complete the reading plan on page 44.

☐ Connect with God each day through prayer.

☐ Spend time with God by engaging the devotional experience on page 45.

➡ ⬅ Personal Study

☐ Read and interact with "Jesus Calls Us to Suffer" on page 46.

☐ Read and interact with "Jesus Calls Us to Sacrifice" on page 48.

⬅ ➡ Application

☐ Throughout the week, ask God to reveal any subtle rebellion or attitude in your life that may be keeping you from total submission to Him. Ask for forgiveness and cleansing (see 1 John 1:8-9).

☐ Memorize Philippians 1:29: "For it has been given to you on Christ's behalf not only to believe in Him, but also to suffer for Him."

☐ Be intentional about seeking joy this week. Even as you consider your sufferings in light of the gospel, choose to also enjoy the blessings God has given you.

☐ Be intentional about blessing others this week, as well. Keep an eye open for those who are in the middle of suffering, and take action to demonstrate kindness.

☐ Other:

WORSHIP

READING PLAN

Continue exploring the Book of Acts throughout this week. Use the space provided to record your thoughts and responses as you read.

Day 1
Acts 9:1-19

Day 2
Acts 9:20-43

Day 3
Acts 10:1-16

Day 4
Acts 10:17-48

Day 5
Acts 11:1-18

Day 6
Acts 11:19-30

Day 7
Acts 12:1-25

OUR FRIEND IN SUFFERING

It sounds strange to say, but we receive many blessings because of the suffering Jesus endured. Obviously, the most important of those blessings is being offered a chance to experience forgiveness for our sins and enjoy reconciliation with God in this life—not to mention the promise of eternal life in heaven during the life to come.

But we should not overlook the additional blessings that Jesus' suffering provides us. For example, the fact that Jesus experienced the full breadth of life in our world means He is familiar with everything we experience in our own lives. He can sympathize with our struggles.

That's one of the primary messages in the Book of Hebrews:

> [14] Therefore, since we have a great high priest who has passed through the heavens—Jesus the Son of God—let us hold fast to the confession. [15] For we do not have a high priest who is unable to sympathize with our weaknesses, but One who has been tested in every way as we are, yet without sin. [16] Therefore let us approach the throne of grace with boldness, so that we may receive mercy and find grace to help us at the proper time.
> **HEBREWS 4:14-16**

> [7] During His earthly life, He offered prayers and appeals with loud cries and tears to the One who was able to save Him from death, and He was heard because of His reverence. [8] Though He was God's Son, He learned obedience through what He suffered. [9] After He was perfected, He became the source of eternal salvation for all who obey Him.
> **HEBREWS 5:7-9**

Take a moment to pray and thank Jesus for the suffering He endured on your behalf.

As you contemplate the reality of Jesus' suffering, allow yourself to be vulnerable and honest about your own struggles. Ask for guidance on how to continue living for God's glory even during suffering.

JESUS CALLS US TO SUFFER

It's important to understand that disciples of Jesus haven't cornered the market on suffering. All people suffer. And yet it is true that Christians should differ from the rest of the world in terms of their response to suffering. While many people suffer hopelessly, desperately, or bitterly, Christians suffer purposefully.

Specifically, we suffer for the spread of the gospel and for the advancement of good.

How have your responses to suffering changed throughout the different phases of your life?

The apostle Paul is perhaps the greatest example we have in the Bible of suffering for the spread of the gospel. Paul's writings proclaim to believers of all ages that not only have we been given the glorious gift of belief in Christ, but we've also been endowed with the privilege of suffering for Him (see Phil. 1:29). While we never suffer to redeem the world—that's already been accomplished by Christ—we do suffer as part of our efforts to reach the world with the gospel message.

Read the following passages of Scripture and record what they teach about suffering for the spread of the gospel.

Philippians 3:7-9

Colossians 1:24-26

2 Timothy 1:8-12

Paul was willing to go anywhere and to suffer any persecution for the privilege of sharing God's message about Christ. For this Paul was beaten, stoned, shipwrecked, imprisoned, sleep deprived, hungry, thirsty, cold, and without adequate clothing (see 2 Cor. 11:24-28). Eventually, he was martyred.

Read Philippians 1:12-18. How would you summarize Paul's conclusions about his own suffering?

When Paul wrote the Book of Philippians, he was a prisoner in Rome. He'd been labeled as a criminal, and he knew such a label could cause others to feel ashamed of him or withdraw from him—or worse, withdraw from active participation in the church.

Paul wanted the church at Philippi to have the proper perspective on the trouble he was experiencing. It wasn't something to be ashamed of or discouraged about. He wanted them to know not only that God was at work in the circumstance of his incarceration, but *how* God was at work. He wanted them to understand how God uses our sufferings—the dangerous and stressful and heartbreaking and life-threatening circumstances in our lives—to spread the gospel to those who don't know Him and to strengthen others who would become more emboldened to speak up about Him.

God can also use your suffering as a means to bring about good in your life and in the lives of others. We don't always like to think about it, but it's true. Whatever God allows to come upon you, He also determines what its use will be in drawing others to Himself and His purposes. The circumstances in your life that have hindered you, bothered you, or frustrated you may actually be magnifying His presence and power in the eyes of those surrounding you. Knowing that doesn't make those circumstances any more fun, but it can help you endure suffering with purpose and resolve.

When have you seen personal suffering result in something good?

Read Philippians 1:21-30. What principles does Paul offer in these verses for enduring suffering with purpose?

As we live out our faith to the best of our abilities, we will experience suffering. Yet, we need not be broken or crushed by the weight of that suffering. Through God's power, we can endure it. Better still, we can live purposefully in the knowledge that our suffering may be used by God to spread the message of the gospel and to advance the cause of good in this world.

 **PERSONAL STUDY**

JESUS CALLS US TO SACRIFICE

There's no way to avoid the truth: Living as disciples of Jesus will require us to make sacrifices. And let's be clear, we're not talking about vague or general sacrifices, such as giving up the pleasure of immorality or releasing the opportunity to be filthy rich. Instead, the sacrifices we make to follow Jesus will be both real and concrete.

Read the following passages of Scripture and record what they teach about making sacrifices in order to follow Christ.

Matthew 10:37-39

Matthew 16:24-27

Luke 9:57-62

Luke 14:31-33

Let's dig deeper into the specific types of sacrifices required to follow Jesus.

First, followers of Jesus must sacrifice possessions. While God does not forbid us from having things, He does want to be sure that *things* don't have *us*. To ensure that God has first place in our hearts, we must untie our affections from the things we own. We must be able to part with material possessions and wealth whenever God leads us to do so.

What are some of your most prized possessions?

Next, followers of Jesus must sacrifice relationships. God will have no rivals for our affections. If we're ever forced to choose between honoring God and honoring our loved ones, we must be ready to choose God unequivocally. Those who would stand in the way of God's interests in our lives or try to discourage us from obeying Him are to be denied the authority to dictate our direction. God is our most sacred relationship, and God alone.

> *What symptoms indicate that one of your personal relationships is taking precedence over your relationship with God?*

In addition, followers of Jesus must sacrifice their plans. There will be times when following Christ requires us to sacrifice our plans in favor of God's plans. He reserves the right to change any of our plans, including our family plans, vacation plans, education plans, retirement plans, financial plans, and even our lunch plans. Followers of Christ humbly allow God to order their steps, giving Him authority over every plan (see Jas. 4:13-15). We submit our intentions to Him each day, surrender our way of doing things to His way, and submit our ambitions and future goals to Him.

> *How will you intentionally submit your short-term and long-term plans to God?*

Finally, followers of Jesus must sacrifice their positions. Surrendering position means being ready to descend from whatever rank we think we've achieved or rise from whatever rest we think we've earned in order to fulfill God's present agenda. It involves relinquishing any honor or role we have, instead yielding to Christ who is to be honored above us (see John 3:30). It involves refusing to use our God-given role in the body of Christ or our social status for personal advantage, but only for the public good as a servant to others (see Luke 22:27).

> *What steps can you take to prepare yourself for any change of position, location, or status that God may require of you?*

WE DIE WITH CHRIST

Death to self is the first step in following Jesus.

REFLECT

In the previous session, we explored the amazing truth that Jesus willingly suffered and sacrificed Himself in order to provide a way for humanity to experience reconciliation with God. We also saw that choosing to follow Jesus as His disciples means embracing our own calls to suffer and sacrifice—all in service of proclaiming the message of the gospel and advancing God's kingdom in this world.

Now it's time to switch the focus of this resource. We've seen that Christ came to us, that He came with a mission, and that He willingly came to die on our behalf. Beginning with this session's material, we'll take a deeper look at what it means for us to follow a similar pattern.

Which of the assignments did you explore this week? How did it go?

What did you learn or experience while reading the Bible?

What questions would you like to ask?

PRAY

Stop for a moment to pray, either individually or as a group:

- Take a moment to reflect silently on the first half of this resource. Share with God what you've learned about yourself and about His Word.

- Thank God for the chance to connect with Jesus and the reality of His sacrifice through your own experience of dying to self.

- Ask the Holy Spirit to reveal anything that might be hindering your walk with the Lord Jesus Christ.

INTRODUCTION

How often do people think about death? Or, how often should people think about death? The answer to those questions can change based on your perspective.

When you think about it from a personal point of view, death is a once-in-a-lifetime experience. All people die, of course, but we only experience death once—and only at the very end of our lives. Therefore, many people rarely think about death. It seems so far off.

When you think about these questions from a global point of view, however, death may seem very near. After all, more than 150,000 people die every day around the world—and more than 50 million people die each year. So, it may also be natural for people to think about death all the time.

How often do you think about death?

What emotions do you typically experience when you think about death?

Strangely enough, it makes sense for disciples of Jesus to think about death more than others in the world. That's because death is exactly what it costs to follow Christ. This cost typically does not include physical death in Western society—although even today there are many martyrs for the cause of Christ around the world.

Instead, the cost of following Jesus involves death to self. As we saw in the previous session, we must lay down control of our lives in order to take up our crosses and follow Christ. We must sacrifice our own plans and priorities in order to follow and obey Him as our Lord.

As we'll see in this session, our experience of dying to self is both a one-time phenomenon and an ongoing requirement.

KNOW THE STORY

Luke records in chapter 14 of his Gospel that large crowds were following Jesus seemingly for the wrong reasons. They had been amazed by His miracles—feeding the multitudes, healing the sick, casting out demons, and so on—but they weren't fully committed to His mission. That's when Jesus gave them something new to think about:

²⁵ Now great crowds were traveling with Him. So He turned and said to them: ²⁶ "If anyone comes to Me and does not hate his own father and mother, wife and children, brothers and sisters—yes, and even his own life—he cannot be My disciple. ²⁷ Whoever does not bear his own cross and come after Me cannot be My disciple.

²⁸ "For which of you, wanting to build a tower, doesn't first sit down and calculate the cost to see if he has enough to complete it? ²⁹ Otherwise, after he has laid the foundation and cannot finish it, all the onlookers will begin to make fun of him, ³⁰ saying, 'This man started to build and wasn't able to finish.'

³¹ "Or what king, going to war against another king, will not first sit down and decide if he is able with 10,000 to oppose the one who comes against him with 20,000? ³² If not, while the other is still far off, he sends a delegation and asks for terms of peace. ³³ In the same way, therefore, every one of you who does not say good-bye to all his possessions cannot be My disciple."
LUKE 14:25-33

How might you have reacted if you heard these words as part of the crowd following Jesus?

How would you summarize Jesus' statements in verses 28-32?

UNPACK THE STORY

DEATH TO SELF IS NECESSARY

It seems to be human nature to react negatively when people demand us to do something. We naturally rebel or resist when given orders. Instead, we prefer a situation where our needs and desires are met first. Even then, we like to be asked nicely. If those conditions are met, and if we're asked in a manner acceptable to us, we'll consider it.

This is not the way of Jesus. In fact, the only thing Jesus wants from us is everything. Notice Jesus' three uses of the word *cannot* in Luke 14:

In order to follow Christ, you must be willing to die to self so that you can live for Him.

- *"If anyone comes to Me and does not hate his own father and mother, wife and children, brothers and sisters—yes, and even his own life—he cannot be My disciple" (v. 26).* This a comparative phrase that basically means our love and devotion to Christ comes absolutely first and above any other human relationship. Our allegiance to Christ makes any other allegiance utterly insignificant.

- *"Whoever does not bear his own cross and come after Me cannot be My disciple" (v. 27).* What does it mean to bear your own cross? Very simply it means that you must die to self. Jesus died on the cross for us, and in order to truly follow Him we must follow Him in that death. We must die to our desires, plans, and priorities.

- *"In the same way, therefore, every one of you who does not say good-bye to all his possessions cannot be My disciple" (v. 33).* This is not a comparative analogy. This is not symbolism. When you follow Jesus, you own nothing and possess nothing—except Jesus.

What questions or concerns come to mind when you read the above list? Why?

How should the above verses influence our daily routines as followers of Christ?

In order to follow Christ, you must be willing to die to self so that you can live for Him. This is the foundation for life as His disciple.

DEATH TO SELF BRINGS LIFE IN CHRIST

There are really two ways we experience death as followers of Jesus. The first is the death of our "old selves":

> [19] For through the law I have died to the law, so that I might live for God. I have been crucified with Christ [20] and I no longer live, but Christ lives in me. The life I now live in the body, I live by faith in the Son of God, who loved me and gave Himself for me.
> **GALATIANS 2:19-20**

This death is what we often refer to as *salvation*. It's a one-time event through which we become a "new creation" (2 Cor. 5:17). The old is gone, and the new has come. Not surprisingly, this form of dying is the easier of the two.

What benefits have you experienced through the process of dying with Christ?

The second way we experience death as followers of Jesus is through the process of dying to self. And *process* is an important word because—unlike the experience of being born again as a new creation—dying to self is not a one-time event. As we've already seen, it's a life-long journey that involves letting go of our plans, priorities, and possessions.

To put it another way, dying to self is the daily discipline of releasing control of our lives and submitting to the control of Christ.

Dying to self is the daily discipline of releasing control of our lives and submitting to the control of Christ.

Do you agree that the one-time event of dying with Christ is easier than the ongoing process of dying to self? Explain.

How have you experienced the struggle of dying to self?

In a strange twist, our experiences with death as followers of Jesus aren't negative or morbid in any way. In fact, dying with Christ and daily dying to ourselves are key landmarks on the pathway toward new life.

ENGAGE

In some ways the concept of dying to self is an abstract one. We don't typically wake up in the morning and say, "I'm going to work on dying to self throughout the day. I'll start right after breakfast." Instead, we participate in the process of dying to self through several personal disciplines that help us relinquish control of our schedules, our resources, our priorities, and so on.

As a group, spend a few minutes reviewing the following spiritual disciplines. Use these questions to help spark discussion for each discipline: (1) How would you describe your experiences with this discipline? (2) How does this discipline help you die to self?

Prayer

Reading God's Word

Fasting

Journaling

Solitude

Keeping the Sabbath

Tithing

PRAYER REQUESTS

....

....

....

....

....

....

....

In addition to studying God's Word, work with your group leader to create a plan for personal study, worship, and application between now and the next session. Select from the following optional activities to match your personal preferences and available time.

⬆ Worship

☑ Read your Bible. Complete the reading plan on page 58.

☐ Connect with God each day through prayer.

☐ Spend time with God by engaging the devotional experience on page 59.

➡⬅ Personal Study

☐ Read and interact with "Dying to Self Clarifies Our Priorities" on page 60.

☐ Read and interact with "Dying to Self Prepares Us to Go on Mission" on page 62.

⬅➡ Application

☐ Start a journal entry this week to record moments when you are confronted with your "old self." Note the different triggers and temptations that make it necessary to once again die to self.

☐ Memorize 2 Corinthians 5:17: "Therefore, if anyone is in Christ, he is a new creation; old things have passed away, and look, new things have come."

☐ Make a list of spiritual goals for the coming month. What are you hoping to achieve or accomplish as part of your new life in Christ?

☐ Look for opportunities to be vulnerable with others regarding your "old self" and old mistakes. There is no need to flaunt the past, of course, but our honesty can often help those who believe disciples of Jesus are required to be perfect.

☐ Other:

WORSHIP

READING PLAN

Continue exploring the Book of Acts throughout this week. Use the space provided to record your thoughts and responses as you read.

Day 1
Acts 13:1-41

Day 2
Acts 13:42-52

Day 3
Acts 14:1-28

Day 4
Acts 15:1-41

Day 5
Acts 16:1-24

Day 6
Acts 16:25-40

Day 7
Acts 17:1-34

BURIED WITH HIM IN BAPTISM

From the earliest days of the church, the ritual of baptism has served as a way for disciples of Jesus to publicly proclaim their faith in Christ as both Savior and Lord. This is a vital practice that should be undertaken by all Christians after their salvation in obedience to the Scriptures. For example:

> [19] Go, therefore, and make disciples of all nations, baptizing them in the name of the Father and of the Son and of the Holy Spirit, [20] teaching them to observe everything I have commanded you. And remember, I am with you always, to the end of the age.
> **MATTHEW 28:19-20**

Baptism is also a perfect picture of what it means to die to self—and a reminder for us to engage in that practice daily:

> [1] What should we say then? Should we continue in sin so that grace may multiply? [2] Absolutely not! How can we who died to sin still live in it? [3] Or are you unaware that all of us who were baptized into Christ Jesus were baptized into His death? [4] Therefore we were buried with Him by baptism into death, in order that, just as Christ was raised from the dead by the glory of the Father, so we too may walk in a new way of life.
> **ROMANS 6:1-4**

Who among your friends and family would benefit from obeying the Scriptures by becoming baptized?

How can you take full advantage of the baptism services in your church as times to worship God?

What do you appreciate most about the chance to "walk in a new way of life"?

DYING TO SELF CLARIFIES OUR PRIORITIES

What's your main priority in life? Followers of Jesus know that God *should* be their primary priority, but it's always helpful to review the recent trajectory of your life and make sure that is the case.

For example, have you funneled a great deal of your time and energy into acquiring money? Or possessions? Do you often dream about achieving fame—or idolize those who have achieved it? Have you based your concept of self-worth on another human being? Or on your position or status as a professional? Do you strive for power or spend a lot of energy seeking to be in control? All of these have proven effective in usurping God's place as the primary priority in our lives.

How would you describe your primary goal or priority in recent months?

What are some signs or symptoms that appear in your life when you begin drifting away from God as your main priority?

As we've seen throughout this session, regaining a focus on dying to self is an excellent way to elevate God and His kingdom as our primary focus. The Scriptures also make it clear that dying to self is a necessary element in moving away from the sinful habits and patterns described above:

> ² Set your minds on what is above, not on what is on the earth. ³ For you have died, and your life is hidden with the Messiah in God. ⁴ When the Messiah, who is your life, is revealed, then you also will be revealed with Him in glory. ⁵ Therefore, put to death what belongs to your worldly nature: sexual immorality, impurity, lust, evil desire, and greed, which is idolatry. ⁶ Because of these, God's wrath comes on the disobedient, ⁷ and you once walked in these things when you were living in them. ⁸ But now you must also put away all the following: anger, wrath, malice, slander, and filthy language from your mouth. ⁹ Do not lie to one another, since you have put off the old self with its practices ¹⁰ and have put on the new self.
> **COLOSSIANS 3:2-10**

What's your initial reaction when reading this passage?

What are some habits or practices that need to be "put to death" in your everyday life?

What are some habits or practices that help you "put on the new self"?

Before Christ, you did what you wanted. Before Christ, you traveled where you wanted. Before Christ, you made the final decisions in every aspect of your life—or at least you thought you did. Now that you've experienced Christ, you have a new Master. And the consistent call from Scripture is that you embrace His authority to set the plan for your life.

Read the following passages of Scripture and record what they teach about the process and benefits of dying to self.

Romans 12:1-2

Galatians 5:22-26

2 Timothy 2:8-13

To follow Jesus as Lord means that we die to everything we want and seek to discover and obey everything He wants. It means Christ has the final say in the affairs and direction of our lives. He is our Savior, and He is our Lord because ultimately He is the King of kings and Lord of lords.

DYING TO SELF PREPARES US TO GO ON MISSION

Take a moment to review the major themes you've covered so far in this study:

- **Session 1:** Jesus Christ is our salvation. His disciples serve as witnesses to that salvation.
- **Session 2:** Jesus came to serve God and set us free. Jesus calls us to serve God and serve others.
- **Session 3:** Jesus suffered and sacrificed. Jesus calls us to suffer and sacrifice for others.

You can see the pattern that's been developing throughout the study. Whenever God reaches into our world to bless us in some way, He calls us not to hoard that blessing, but to extend it outward to others.

What are some of the primary ways God has blessed you?

What steps have you taken to extend those blessings to others?

The same principle holds true for the blessing (and responsibility) we've described in this session as dying to self. We've seen that dying to self helps us maintain our focus on God and keep Him as our primary priority. The apostle Paul reminded us of that truth in the Book of 2 Corinthians:

> [14] For Christ's love compels us, since we have reached this conclusion: If One died for all, then all died. [15] And He died for all so that those who live should no longer live for themselves, but for the One who died for them and was raised.
> **2 CORINTHIANS 5:14-15**

How do these verses connect with the concept of dying to self?

But we must remember that the purpose of dying to self goes beyond simply our own benefit. Indeed, when we set ourselves in line with God, we join Him in His mission to redeem the world. Look at how Paul continued his train of thought:

¹⁶ From now on, then, we do not know anyone in a purely human way. Even if we have known Christ in a purely human way, yet now we no longer know Him in this way. ¹⁷ Therefore, if anyone is in Christ, he is a new creation; old things have passed away, and look, new things have come. ¹⁸ Everything is from God, who reconciled us to Himself through Christ and gave us the ministry of reconciliation: ¹⁹ That is, in Christ, God was reconciling the world to Himself, not counting their trespasses against them, and He has committed the message of reconciliation to us. ²⁰ Therefore, we are ambassadors for Christ, certain that God is appealing through us. We plead on Christ's behalf, "Be reconciled to God."
2 CORINTHIANS 5:16-20

Make no mistake: dying to self *is* an incredible blessing. Have you considered what a privilege it is to live as a "new creation" (v. 17)? To know that your old self has "passed away" and that "new things have come"? You have been reconciled to God! You are part of His kingdom once again.

Therefore, take pains to prevent yourself from hoarding that blessing.

As disciples of Jesus Christ, God has given us "the ministry of reconciliation" (v. 18). Of course, we don't have the ability or the authority to reconcile people to God—only He can accomplish that. Yet He has enlisted us to help in the process by serving as agents of the gospel. To use Paul's phrasing, we are "ambassadors for Christ" who have a specific role in proclaiming the good news of salvation. "We plead on Christ's behalf, 'Be reconciled to God'" (v. 20).

How confident do you feel in your role as an ambassador for Christ?

1	2	3	4	5	6	7	8	9	10
Not confident									Very confident

What specific steps can you take to be more active in proclaiming the gospel message this week?

WE GO WITH CHRIST

Jesus sends us out as disciples
in order to make disciples.

REFLECT

In the previous session, we explored the necessary practice of dying to self as a follower of Jesus. We saw that death to self means setting aside our priorities, plans, dreams, and desires—all for the sake of taking Jesus' priorities, plans, dreams, and desires as our own. We also learned that death to self is both a one-time event and a daily discipline.

Before we begin a deeper exploration of our mission as followers of Jesus, take a moment to discuss your experiences in recent days.

Which of the assignments did you explore this week? How did it go?

What did you learn or experience while reading the Bible?

What questions would you like to ask?

PRAY

Stop for a moment to pray, either individually or as a group:

- Thank God that He has blessed with you a mission and a purpose that carry weight, both in this world and in the next.

- Ask the Holy Spirit to give you eyes to see the world like He sees the world.

- Proclaim your willingness to serve on mission as an ambassador for Jesus Christ.

INTRODUCTION

On September 12, 1962, President John F. Kennedy delivered a landmark speech at Rice University in Houston, during which he reminded his listeners about the American goal to land a man on the moon and return him safely. Here's part of what the president said:

> We choose to go to the moon. We choose to go to the moon in this decade and do the other things, not because they are easy, but because they are hard—because that goal will serve to organize and measure the best of our energies and skills, because that challenge is one that we are willing to accept, one we are unwilling to postpone, and one which we intend to win. It is for these reasons that I regard the decision last year to shift our efforts in space from low to high gear as among the most important decisions that will be made during my incumbency in the office of the Presidency.[1]

This decision to go to the moon required enormous sacrifice, hard work, and courage. At its peak, the Apollo program employed hundreds of thousands of people and required the support of thousands more industrial firms and universities. In financial terms, it cost the U. S. government more than $25.4 billion to land the first astronauts on the moon.[2]

And it worked. On July 20, 1969, the mission was completed when Neil Armstrong stepped off the lunar lander and announced, "That's one small step for man ... one giant leap for mankind." The mission motivated and guided a nation to accomplish something that is still amazing even by today's standards.

In your opinion, what are some of the most impressive accomplishments in human history?

The right mission can inspire people in amazing ways and motivate them to go above and beyond in completing whatever tasks they receive. President Kennedy's mission sparked the imagination and the perspiration of an entire country.

Yet, even that remarkable achievement of human effort pales in comparison to the mission Jesus has given His disciples.

KNOW THE STORY

The Bible records Jesus' mission in several passages, many of which we've explored throughout this resource. In each case, it's clear that Jesus' mission offers a worthy and inspirational vision for His followers—one that will require enormous sacrifice, hard work, and courage on our part.

The most famous expression of Jesus' mission can be found at the end of Matthew's Gospel in one of Jesus' final words to His disciples. Verses 18-20 are called the Great Commission:

[16] The 11 disciples traveled to Galilee, to the mountain where Jesus had directed them. [17] When they saw Him, they worshiped, but some doubted.

[18] Then Jesus came near and said to them, "All authority has been given to Me in heaven and on earth. [19] Go, therefore, and make disciples of all nations, baptizing them in the name of the Father and of the Son and of the Holy Spirit, [20] teaching them to observe everything I have commanded you. And remember, I am with you always, to the end of the age."
MATTHEW 28:16-20

Take note of verse 17. When have you doubted or been confused by your place in Jesus' mission?

What helps you feel confident about Jesus and His mission?

This was the mission statement that guided a group of ordinary, untrained men as they launched the church and laid a foundation for success from which we still benefit today. Yet, this mission wasn't delivered *only* to the disciples of Jesus' day. The above verses also describe our primary mission as followers of Christ within the modern church.

In other words, these verses are a critical summary of your mission as an individual disciple of Jesus Christ.

UNPACK THE STORY

JESUS' MISSION IS ACCOMPLISHED

We saw back in Session 2 of this resource that Jesus began His public ministry by announcing the major points of His mission for the world. Jesus shocked the people of His hometown by proclaiming Himself as the Messiah and promising good news and freedom from suffering to all who needed it.

Look at Luke 4:16-20. How has your understanding of Jesus' mission developed throughout this study?

There is a sense, then, in which Jesus' mission for the world has already been accomplished. In obedience to the Father, Jesus came into our world not only to preach the good news and teach people about the kingdom of heaven, but ultimately to offer Himself as a sacrifice for the atonement of our sins.

That mission is over. On the cross, Jesus finished what He came to do:

> When Jesus had received the sour wine, He said, "It is finished!" Then bowing His head, He gave up His spirit.
> **JOHN 19:30**

On the cross, Jesus finished what He came to do.

Yet, there is also a sense in which Jesus' mission is still ongoing. There is still work to be done—still people across the world yearning for freedom and release from suffering. More importantly, there are still people who need to hear the good news of the gospel, understand that news, and take action to accept the gift of forgiveness offered to them.

That's where we come in:

> Jesus said to them again, "Peace to you! As the Father has sent Me, I also send you."
> **JOHN 20:21**

When have you felt most passionate about evangelism?

OUR CONTINUING MISSION IS CRITICAL

When we explore the Great Commission verse-by-verse, we find three important truths that guide our mission as followers of Christ:

1. Our mission is to make disciples. Don't miss the primary command in Jesus' commission: "Go, therefore, and make disciples of all nations ..." (Matt. 28:19). Our first step in making disciples is to "go" and engage the world, rather than sitting back and waiting for the world to come to church. There are no set rules for what it means to "make disciples," but the process does involve proclaiming the gospel, baptizing those who follow Christ, and continually teaching them what it means to live as His disciples.

2. Our mission is based on Jesus' authority. Jesus' first declaration to His disciples was critical: "All authority has been given to Me in heaven and on earth" (v. 18). We don't make disciples because it's the right thing to do, or even because we want people to go to heaven. Instead, we make disciples because Jesus—the Lord, Master, and King of all the universe—has commanded us to do so.

3. Our mission includes Jesus' presence. Many people overlook verse 20 when they reference the Great Commission, but Jesus' final words are crucial: "And remember, I am with you always, to the end of the age." Not only do we engage our mission under Christ's authority, but also within His presence. We're not called to go it alone or left to figure things out for ourselves. Instead, we have the privilege of daily encounters with Jesus even as we work to achieve the mission He gave us.

How would you describe what it means to "make disciples"?

What questions would you like to ask about the process of making disciples?

In what areas would you like to improve as a disciple maker?

We are called to make disciples of Jesus Christ— to play a part in developing people who think like Jesus, act like Jesus, and love like Jesus.

In Matthew 28 and throughout the New Testament, our mission is clear. We are called to make disciples of Jesus Christ—to play a part in developing people who think like Jesus, act like Jesus, and love like Jesus. This is our great work in the world, even as we strive to think, act, and love like Jesus in our own lives.

ENGAGE

We are commanded to make disciples. That's our mission. But what does that phrase actually mean? How do we go about the process of making disciples? Take a few moments to address those questions as a group.

Gather in smaller groups of two or three to discuss the following questions. Be open to sharing both your life experiences and your thoughts on what you've learned throughout this resource.

What have been the major landmarks in your development as a disciple of Jesus?

Who has been influential in your growth as a disciple?

What obstacles have hindered your growth as a disciple?

How would you describe your current plan for making disciples?

PRAYER REQUESTS

....

....

....

....

....

....

....

....

....

....

1. er.jsc.nasa.gov/seh/ricetalk.htm, accessed 05/13/15.
2. Congress, House of Representatives, Committee on Science and Astronautics (1973). 1974 NASA Authorization Hearings (Hearing on H.R. 4567). Washington, D.C.: 93rd Congress, first session. OCLC 23229007.

In addition to studying God's Word, work with your group leader to create a plan for personal study, worship, and application between now and the next session. Select from the following optional activities to match your personal preferences and available time.

⬆ Worship

☑ Read your Bible. Complete the reading plan on page 72.

☐ Connect with God each day through prayer.

☐ Spend time with God by engaging the devotional experience on page 73.

➡ ⬅ Personal Study

☐ Read and interact with "Three Important Participles" on page 74.

☐ Read and interact with "Five Critical Commissions" on page 76.

⬅ ➡ Application

☐ Continue to pray daily for friends, family members, and acquaintances in your sphere of influence who are not yet disciples of Jesus. Pray for each person by name.

☐ Make sure your efforts to make disciples are fueled by Jesus' presence and authority. Set aside at least an hour this week to spend in God's presence through prayer and meditation on His Word.

☐ Commit to sharing the gospel message with at least one person this week.

☐ Memorize Acts 1:8: "But you will receive power when the Holy Spirit has come on you, and you will be My witnesses in Jerusalem, in all Judea and Samaria, and to the ends of the earth."

☐ Other:

WORSHIP

READING PLAN

Continue exploring the Book of Acts throughout this week. Use the space provided to record your thoughts and responses as you read.

Day 1
Acts 18:1-28

Day 2
Acts 19:1-20

Day 3
Acts 19:21-41

Day 4
Acts 20:1-38

Day 5
Acts 21:1-40

Day 6
Acts 22:1-30

Day 7
Acts 23:1-35

VINES AND BRANCHES

The Great Commission is not a suggestion. It's a command. It's Jesus sending out His disciples for a specific mission and purpose. And yet it's a command that contains an important promise: "And remember, I am with you always, to the end of the age" (Matt. 28:20).

Certainly, we should receive comfort from the promise of Jesus' presence. Yet, we will struggle in carrying out our mission if we think of Jesus' presence as an added bonus or a supplement to our own abilities. The truth is, we cannot do anything productive outside of Jesus' presence and power. We are entirely dependent on Him even as we carry out His mission.

Jesus spoke about this reality in the Gospel of John:

> 4 Remain in Me, and I in you. Just as a branch is unable to produce fruit by itself unless it remains on the vine, so neither can you unless you remain in Me.
>
> 5 I am the vine; you are the branches. The one who remains in Me and I in him produces much fruit, because you can do nothing without Me. 6 If anyone does not remain in Me, he is thrown aside like a branch and he withers. They gather them, throw them into the fire, and they are burned. 7 If you remain in Me and My words remain in you, ask whatever you want and it will be done for you. 8 My Father is glorified by this: that you produce much fruit and prove to be My disciples.
> **JOHN 15:4-8**

How do you actively seek Jesus' presence each day?

What disciplines or practices help you become more aware of (and more reliant on) Jesus' presence?

THREE IMPORTANT PARTICIPLES

One of the amazing characteristics of the Bible is that the deeper you dig into the text, the more you will find and the more profoundly you will be changed. The Scriptures are a bottomless well constantly flowing with the water of life. With that in mind, we can glean some more information about the Great Commission when we take a closer look at the structure of the text itself—specifically verses 18-20:

> ¹⁸ Then Jesus came near and said to them, "All authority has been given to Me in heaven and on earth. ¹⁹ Go, therefore, and make disciples of all nations, baptizing them in the name of the Father and of the Son and of the Holy Spirit, ²⁰ teaching them to observe everything I have commanded you. And remember, I am with you always, to the end of the age."
> **MATTHEW 28:18-20**

The Great Commission is essentially a single command surrounded by three participles. In case you're not familiar with that term, a participle is a verb used to modify another element in a sentence. "Going" (or "go"), "baptizing," and "teaching" are the three participles contained in the Great Commission. Each one offers a helpful explanation of Jesus' command to "make disciples."

Going. Without being too technical, the word "go" found in modern English Bibles wasn't structured as a command in the original Greek language of the New Testament. Instead, the term was written as a participle that means "in your going" or "after you have gone." This term is directly connected to the focal point of the sentence, which is "make disciples."

In other words, "going" is a necessary element of making disciples. We can't help others encounter Jesus until we direct our focus outward, away from ourselves. Disciples of Jesus follow His example by going—across the street, across the city, across the country, and across the world—in order to show and share the good news.

What opportunities do you have to go on Jesus' behalf in your local church and community?

What opportunities do you have to go across the world?

Baptizing. The practice of baptism takes place after salvation as an illustration of what happens when we become disciples of Jesus. In that moment of conversion, we join with Jesus in both His death and His resurrection—we die to our old selves and begin a new life for Christ and His kingdom.

Baptism is more than a symbol, however. It also serves as a public declaration of allegiance to Christ—a declaration Jesus commanded us to take in the Great Commission. Therefore, when we encourage new disciples to be baptized, we are encouraging a strong first step of obedience on their journey as followers of Jesus.

What action steps come to mind when you think about the importance of baptism?

Teaching. The final participle is "teaching," which involves both intellectual instruction and practical training. If Jesus had commanded us only to teach new disciples everything He commanded us, we would be free to focus solely on the doctrines of the Christian faith. We could preach and teach about justification, sanctification, the Trinity, the fall, and much more—all without the burden of having to actually do anything.

But Jesus commanded us to make disciples by "teaching them *to observe* everything I have commanded you" (v. 20, emphasis added). We've been commanded not just to teach disciples about the practices of the Christian faith, but also to model those practices. We have a duty to help disciples of Jesus—ourselves included—learn how to take action based on what we've been taught.

Who has been influential in teaching you about Christian principles and practices?

Who has been influential in showing you how to incorporate those principles and practices in your everyday life?

Jesus accomplished His mission on earth. Thankfully, He goes with us as we seek to make disciples for His glory and in obedience to His command.

FIVE CRITICAL COMMISSIONS

We've seen that the Great Commission in Matthew 28:19-20 serves as a helpful summary of our mission as disciples of Jesus. But it's not the only helpful summary. In fact, there are five commissions recorded in the early portions of the New Testament—all given by Jesus to His disciples.

All five commissions are worth exploring. Review the four additional commissions outlined in the following Scripture passages, beginning with the Book of Mark:

> ¹⁴ Later, He appeared to the Eleven themselves as they were reclining at the table. He rebuked their unbelief and hardness of heart, because they did not believe those who saw Him after He had been resurrected. ¹⁵ Then He said to them, "Go into all the world and preach the gospel to the whole creation. ¹⁶ Whoever believes and is baptized will be saved, but whoever does not believe will be condemned."
> **MARK 16:14-16**

What are your initial impressions of these verses?

How do these verses compare and contrast with the Great Commission?

Next comes Jesus' commission near the end of Luke's Gospel, although these verses serve primarily as a reminder for the disciples to carry out everything Jesus had already said:

> ⁴⁵ Then He opened their minds to understand the Scriptures. ⁴⁶ He also said to them, "This is what is written: The Messiah would suffer and rise from the dead the third day, ⁴⁷ and repentance for forgiveness of sins would be proclaimed in His name to all the nations, beginning at Jerusalem. ⁴⁸ You are witnesses of these things. ⁴⁹ And look, I am sending you what My Father promised. As for you, stay in the city until you are empowered from on high."
> **LUKE 24:45-49**

*Jesus "opened their minds to understand the Scriptures" (v. 45).
How has the Bible guided your mission as a disciple of Jesus?*

In Luke 24 Jesus made reference to sending "what My Father promised," meaning the Holy Spirit. The final chapter of John's Gospel also highlights the Spirit's role in empowering our mission:

> [21] Jesus said to them again, "Peace to you! As the Father has sent Me, I also send you." [22] After saying this, He breathed on them and said, "Receive the Holy Spirit. [23] If you forgive the sins of any, they are forgiven them; if you retain the sins of any, they are retained."
> **JOHN 20:21-23**

How has the Holy Spirit fueled your efforts to serve Jesus?

Finally, the first chapter in the Book of Acts contains Jesus' final words to His disciples before His ascension into heaven:

> [7] He said to them, "It is not for you to know times or periods that the Father has set by His own authority. [8] But you will receive power when the Holy Spirit has come on you, and you will be My witnesses in Jerusalem, in all Judea and Samaria, and to the ends of the earth."
> **ACTS 1:7-8**

What obstacles are currently hindering the gospel message from being fully proclaimed "to the ends of the earth"?

What action steps will you take in the coming weeks based on your contemplation of these passages?

WE GO TOGETHER WITH CHRIST

Jesus sends us out as a community
of disciples in order to make disciples

REFLECT

In the previous session we took a deeper look at our mission to make disciples as individual followers of Jesus. We saw that making disciples is a command, not a suggestion. And we learned that the process of disciple making involves going out into the world, baptizing those who encounter Christ, and teaching them how to practice the fundamental truths of God's Word.

In this session, we'll explore what it means to make disciples, not only as individuals but also as a corporate body of Christ. First, take a moment to discuss your experiences in recent days.

Which of the assignments did you explore this week? How did it go?

What did you learn or experience while reading the Bible?

What questions would you like to ask?

PRAY

Stop for a moment to pray, either individually or as a group:

- Thank God for making you part of a community within the body of Christ.

- Ask the Father to help you maintain a connection with Jesus as the Head of that body.

- Affirm your desire to join with the full body of Christ in order to engage His mission of making disciples.

INTRODUCTION

You may have noticed that visiting the doctor involves a predictable routine—especially at the beginning of the appointment. Most physicians begin by seeking to answer the same series of questions in order to get a broad assessment of your physical health:

- How tall are you?
- How much do you weigh?
- What's your blood pressure?
- Do you have any allergies?
- Do you smoke?
- Are you currently taking any prescription medications?
- Are you currently experiencing pain or discomfort?

Through hundreds of years of study, the medical profession has developed certain base-line measurements and acceptable criteria that help doctors perceive when a body may be out of alignment. The human body is intricately designed and amazingly complex, yet answering a few relatively simple questions can reveal a great deal of information about a person's overall health.

During what periods of your life have you felt the most healthy or health-conscious?

What are some important steps for promoting physical health?

Throughout the New Testament, the worldwide church is described as "the body of Christ" (see 1 Cor. 12:27, for example). Every individual disciple of Jesus has been included in that body, along with every local church and congregation. Jesus Himself governs and directs the church as its Head.

Interestingly, in the same way that a few basic questions can help evaluate a physical body, there are key factors that help us evaluate the health and productivity of the church as the body of Christ. As we'll see in this session, we know the church is healthy when disciples of Jesus work together in a corporate effort to obey Him and make more disciples.

KNOW THE STORY

The concept of the church existing as the body of Christ can be found throughout the New Testament. However, the writings of the apostle Paul offer the deepest and most direct references to that idea—including both how we should understand the body and why it's important for us to do so.

The following passage from 1 Corinthians is a helpful example of Paul's views on the body of Christ. As you read, pay attention to the strength and confidence of his words.

[12] For as the body is one and has many parts, and all the parts of that body, though many, are one body—so also is Christ. [13] For we were all baptized by one Spirit into one body—whether Jews or Greeks, whether slaves or free—and we were all made to drink of one Spirit. [14] So the body is not one part but many. [15] If the foot should say, "Because I'm not a hand, I don't belong to the body," in spite of this it still belongs to the body. [16] And if the ear should say, "Because I'm not an eye, I don't belong to the body," in spite of this it still belongs to the body. [17] If the whole body were an eye, where would the hearing be? If the whole body were an ear, where would the sense of smell be? [18] But now God has placed each one of the parts in one body just as He wanted. [19] And if they were all the same part, where would the body be? [20] Now there are many parts, yet one body.

[27] Now you are the body of Christ, and individual members of it.
1 CORINTHIANS 12:12-20,27

How would you summarize the different principles Paul communicated in these verses?

Why is it important for all disciples of Jesus to understand and apply these verses?

As usual, Paul didn't mince words when he wrote the above passage. He spoke clearly and confidently. The church is the body of Christ. All disciples are included in that body. Therefore, all disciples have important work to do.

UNPACK THE STORY

WE ARE THE BODY OF CHRIST

One of the more interesting implications of Paul's teaching in 1 Corinthians 12 is that there's no such thing as an isolated disciple of Jesus. It's become popular in recent years for people to proclaim their intention to follow Jesus without connecting themselves to the broader church. According to Paul, however, such a concept is impossible.

To be a disciple of Jesus is to be intricately and intimately involved in the church. The moment we experience salvation, we are grafted into the body of Christ as one more of its "many parts" (v. 12).

How would you describe your experiences with the church over the course of your life?

Not only are you connected with Jesus as part of His body, but you are also positioned in just the right way to accomplish the work to which God has called you.

You are part of the body of Christ, and that is wonderful news. Because even with the church's past mistakes and current faults, Jesus is the Head. You are a part of *His* body, which means you are intimately connected to Him.

Notice this additional promise from God's Word: "But now God has placed each one of the parts in one body *just as He wanted*" (1 Cor. 12:18, emphasis added). Not only are you connected with Jesus as part of His body, but you are also positioned in just the right way to accomplish the work to which God has called you.

You have been specifically and specially designed to serve Jesus as a working member of His body.

Many Christians feel uncertain or unsettled about their place in their local church, which is understandable given that people—even well-meaning disciples of Christ—aren't perfect. Still, Jesus has promised us a place in His body. Therefore, our service in the church becomes a matter of faith more than comfort.

In what ways has God equipped you to serve the church?

WE WORK TOGETHER TO MAKE DISCIPLES

There's no question that being part of the church—both in local congregations and smaller groups—provides a number of benefits. We can find community and friendship in the church, for example. We can find support and encouragement. We can find education and transformational teaching. All of these are wonderful blessings.

But we must always remember that the body of Christ wasn't designed solely to bless the members of that body. Rather, the church exists to accomplish the will of its Head, which is Christ. And it is Christ's will for the church to make disciples.

Look back to the early church, for example:

> [41] So those who accepted his message were baptized, and that day about 3,000 people were added to them. [42] And they devoted themselves to the apostles' teaching, to the fellowship, to the breaking of bread, and to the prayers.
>
> [43] Then fear came over everyone, and many wonders and signs were being performed through the apostles. [44] Now all the believers were together and held all things in common. [45] They sold their possessions and property and distributed the proceeds to all, as anyone had a need. [46] Every day they devoted themselves to meeting together in the temple complex, and broke bread from house to house. They ate their food with a joyful and humble attitude, [47] praising God and having favor with all the people. And every day the Lord added to them those who were being saved.
> **ACTS 2:41-47**

The church exists to accomplish the will of its Head, which is Christ. And it is Christ's will for the church to make disciples.

How do these verses show obedience to the Great Commission?

What are some of the practical ways your group or congregation works toward obeying the Great Commission?

How has the Holy Spirit been leading you to participate in the work of your church?

ENGAGE

It's not always easy for people to work well with others. Even among disciples of Jesus, it can be difficult to set aside our own egos and agendas in order to function as a team. For that reason, it's important for the members of your group to be intentional about finding ways to strive for unity together.

Fortunately, one of the simplest methods for strengthening the bonds within your group is also one of the most effective. That method is prayer. When you and your group members join together to intercede for one another in the presence of God's Spirit, you will experience greater unity. You will develop deeper levels of trust, encouragement, and appreciation.

As a group, spend several minutes sharing about issues or circumstances for which you'd like prayer.

Pray for one another out loud. As each group member prays, the others should focus on mentally echoing his or her statements to God.

Conclude by committing to pray daily for one another by name until the next group gathering.

PRAYER REQUESTS

....

....

....

....

....

....

....

....

....

....

....

In addition to studying God's Word, work with your group leader to create a plan for personal study, worship, and application between now and the next session. Select from the following optional activities to match your personal preferences and available time.

↑ Worship

☑ Read your Bible. Complete the reading plan on page 86.

☐ Connect with God each day through prayer.

☐ Spend time with God by engaging the devotional experience on page 87.

➡ ⬅ Personal Study

☐ Read and interact with "Find Your Place in the Body" on page 88.

☐ Read and interact with "Join the Body in Making Disciples" on page 90.

⬅ ➡ Application

☐ Take out your calendar and review your current involvement with your local church. Are you fully investing yourself as a functioning member of the body of Christ?

☐ Memorize Colossians 1:17-18: "He is before all things, and by Him all things hold together. He is also the head of the body, the church; He is the beginning, the firstborn from the dead, so that He might come to have first place in everything."

☐ Identify a church function or group encounter in the near future to which you can invite friends or family members who need to meet Jesus. Pray for these individuals each day, and be alert for opportunities to make the invitation.

☐ Invite a fellow disciple to join you in a spiritual activity—studying God's Word, memorizing Scripture, prayer, evangelism, fasting, and so on.

☐ Other:

WORSHIP

READING PLAN

Conclude your reading of the Book of Acts this week. Use the space provided to record your thoughts and responses as you read.

Day 1
Acts 24:1-27

Day 2
Acts 25:1-27

Day 3
Acts 26:1-23

Day 4
Acts 26:24-32

Day 5
Acts 27:1-44

Day 6
Acts 28:1-16

Day 7
Acts 28:17-31

CONTENTMENT IN THE BODY

To be included in the body of Christ is a wonderful privilege. We have the chance to serve God even as we enjoy the benefits of community within the church. Yet, there are still obstacles that need to be overcome. There are still areas of sin or misunderstanding that can cause pain for individuals and friction within the church.

One of those obstacles is the presence of discontentment. To be frank, it's common for disciples of Jesus to feel dissatisfied about their role within the church. Sometimes this is a mild desire for more recognition, more influence, or less stressful responsibilities. Other times our discontentment becomes a full-fledged root of bitterness and pride.

In either case, the apostle Paul was clear that a lack of contentment will have dangerous consequences within the body of Christ:

> [12] As the body is one and has many parts, and all the parts of that body, though many, are one body—so also is Christ.
>
> [21] So the eye cannot say to the hand, "I don't need you!" Or again, the head can't say to the feet, "I don't need you!" [22] But even more, those parts of the body that seem to be weaker are necessary. [23] And those parts of the body that we think to be less honorable, we clothe these with greater honor, and our unpresentable parts have a better presentation. [24] But our presentable parts have no need of clothing. Instead, God has put the body together, giving greater honor to the less honorable, [25] so that there would be no division in the body, but that the members would have the same concern for each other. [26] So if one member suffers, all the members suffer with it; if one member is honored, all the members rejoice with it.
> **1 CORINTHIANS 12:12,21-26**

Do you feel content with your role in the body of Christ? Explain.

What disciplines or practices can help you increase your level of contentment as a disciple of Jesus?

FIND YOUR PLACE IN THE BODY

If you've been transformed as a disciple of Jesus Christ, then you are part of His body, the church. Even more, you have a specific role and function as a member of that body—you've been uniquely designed and specially placed to advance the work of the broader church within the community of your local group and congregation.

Therefore, one of the best ways to make sure you're contributing well is to identify your role and function within your church. In what ways have you been gifted? How can you contribute to the life and ministry of your church community? These are questions you've been pondering throughout this session. Thankfully, the apostle Paul highlighted several important roles within the church during his letter to the Christians in Ephesus:

> [11] And He personally gave some to be apostles, some prophets, some evangelists, some pastors and teachers, [12] for the training of the saints in the work of ministry, to build up the body of Christ, [13] until we all reach unity in the faith and in the knowledge of God's Son, growing into a mature man with a stature measured by Christ's fullness. [14] Then we will no longer be little children, tossed by the waves and blown around by every wind of teaching, by human cunning with cleverness in the techniques of deceit. [15] But speaking the truth in love, let us grow in every way into Him who is the head—Christ. [16] From Him the whole body, fitted and knit together by every supporting ligament, promotes the growth of the body for building up itself in love by the proper working of each individual part.
> **EPHESIANS 4:11-16**

What are the roles and functions within the body of Christ mentioned in the above passage?

What are some additional roles and functions carried out by members of your church today?

Notice Paul's emphasis in verse 16 that the body is built up and remains healthy through "the proper working of each individual part." That's you. Every disciple of Jesus has a share in maintaining the health and productivity of the church. More, we have a responsibility to do our part in helping the body of Christ fulfill its mission—a responsibility that includes consequences when we neglect our duty.

Jesus made that clear when He shared the parable of the talents with His disciples.

Read Matthew 25:14-30. How would you summarize the primary theme of Jesus' parable?

What are some recent ways you've invested your talents—your gifts and abilities—in order to make disciples within the body of Christ?

Many people feel hesitant about pouring themselves into the church's mission to make disciples, and there are many reasons for that hesitation. Some simply don't want to give up greater control of their lives. Others aren't willing to let go of cherished possessions or long-held habits. Still, others feel they don't possess the right gifts for making disciples—they don't have the gift of teaching or they don't possess a striking personal testimony.

In the end, all of these excuses boil down to the same thing: disobedience. Our Master has commanded us to work together as His body in order to make disciples for His kingdom. That is our mission.

What you do next is your choice.

How would you describe your specific role within the body of Christ?

What obstacles are currently hindering you from engaging that role to a greater degree?

JOIN THE BODY IN MAKING DISCIPLES

Jesus came to our world with a mission to redeem our world—us included. He became one of us so that He could teach us and model what it means to follow God. He suffered on our behalf. He died as the atonement for our sins. And His glorious resurrection made it possible for all people to join with Him in a new and restored relationship with God.

That was His mission, and He accomplished it.

Jesus gave His disciples a mission as well—one that should drive us each day to expand His kingdom and bring glory to God. Having come to the conclusion of this study, take another look at the mission as He expressed it:

> 18 Then Jesus came near and said to them, "All authority has been given to Me in heaven and on earth. 19 Go, therefore, and make disciples of all nations, baptizing them in the name of the Father and of the Son and of the Holy Spirit, 20 teaching them to observe everything I have commanded you. And remember, I am with you always, to the end of the age."
> **MATTHEW 28:18-20**

How has your understanding of these verses changed or deepened in recent weeks?

In what ways have you actively obeyed Jesus' command to make disciples in recent months?

"Make disciples." That's your mission as an individual follower of Jesus. Yet, you cannot accomplish that mission alone. You need to work as part of the body of Christ if you want to make any progress— let alone make disciples. You need to actively plug yourself into the life of your local church.

With that in mind, use the following assessments and questions to help you continue moving forward in obedience to God and to demonstrate active passion for your mission as a disciple of Christ.

How confident do you feel in your ability to make disciples?

1   2   3   4   5   6   7   8   9   10

Not confident   Very confident

Who are three people you will pray for each day to encounter Jesus in a transformational way?

1.
2.
3.

Who are three current disciples you will pray for each day to continue growing in their maturity and obedience to Christ?

1.
2.
3.

What spiritual disciplines will help you rely on Jesus' presence as you obey the Great Commission?

To what degree are you currently being supported, encouraged, and instructed by other disciples of Jesus?

1   2   3   4   5   6   7   8   9   10

A low degree   A high degree

How will you actively seek encouragement and support from other disciples of Jesus as you work to obey the Great Commission?

If your group is continuing on the *Disciples Path* journey, choose your next study using the chart below or find other discipleship studies at *www.lifeway.com/goadults*

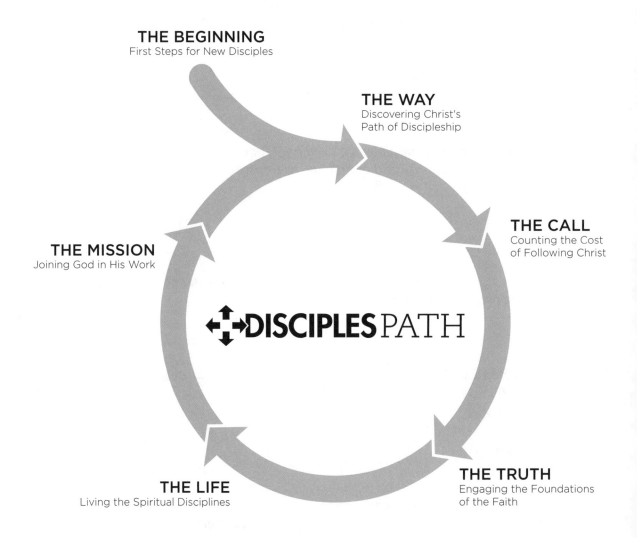

THE BEGINNING
First Steps for New Disciples

THE WAY
Discovering Christ's
Path of Discipleship

THE CALL
Counting the Cost
of Following Christ

THE MISSION
Joining God in His Work

THE TRUTH
Engaging the Foundations
of the Faith

THE LIFE
Living the Spiritual Disciplines

TAKE THE NEXT STEP.

Disciples Path is a series of resources founded on Jesus' model of discipleship. Created by experienced disciple makers across the nation, it is an intentional path of transformational discipleship. While most small-group studies facilitate transformation through relationship and information, these disciple-making resources do it through the principles of modeling, practicing, and multiplying.

- Leaders model a biblical life.
- Disciples follow and practice from the leader.
- Disciples become disciple makers and multiply through *Disciples Path*.

Each of the six studies in the *Disciples Path* series has been written and approved by disciple makers for one-on-one settings as well as small groups. The series includes:

1. THE BEGINNING
Take the first step for a new believer and new disciple.

2. THE WAY
Walk through the Gospels and follow the journey of Jesus and the first disciples.

3. THE CALL
Gain a deeper understanding of what it means to follow Christ in everyday life.

4. THE TRUTH
Dive into the doctrinal truths of biblical discipleship.

5. THE LIFE
Take a deeper look at the essential disciplines and practices of following Christ.

6. THE MISSION
Get equipped for God's mission and discover your role in joining Him in the world.

To learn more or take the next step, visit lifeway.com/disciplespath.

LEADER INSTRUCTIONS

As a group leader or mentor, you have a vital role in the process of discipleship—one that involves both blessing and responsibility. Keep in mind the following guidelines as you faithfully obey the Great Commission.

YOUR GOAL

Remember that your ultimate goal in the discipleship process is spiritual transformation. The best fruit for your efforts as a leader is spiritual growth that results in transformed hearts—both for you and for the disciples under your care.

Remember also that spiritual transformation is most likely to occur when a godly leader applies truth to the heart of a person while that person is in a teachable posture. As the leader, you have direct control over the first two of those conditions; you can also encourage and support disciples as they seek a teachable posture. Take advantage of those opportunities.

YOUR METHODS

Use the following suggestions as you work toward the goal of spiritual transformation.

- **Pray daily.** Studies have shown that leaders who pray every day for the disciples under their care see the most spiritual fruit during the discipleship process. Your ultimate goal is spiritual transformation; therefore, seek the Holy Spirit.

- **Teach information.** This resource contains helpful information on the basic elements of the Christian faith. During group discussions, you'll want to be familiar enough with the content to avoid reading each page verbatim. Highlighting key words or even creating your own bullet points will help you facilitate the time most effectively. Prepare in advance.

- **Seek conversation.** As you lead disciples through the material, seek to engage them in meaningful conversation. To help you, discussion questions have been provided throughout the group portion of each session. These questions provide an opportunity to pause and allow each disciple to react to the teaching. They also allow you as the disciple maker an opportunity to gauge how each person is progressing along the path of discipleship.

- **Model practices.** Many disciples learn best by observing others. Therefore, each session of this resource includes opportunities for you to model the attributes, disciplines, and practices of a growing disciple of Jesus. Take advantage of these opportunities by intentionally showing disciples how to pray, interact with God's Word, worship God, and so on—and by inviting feedback and questions.

May God bless your efforts to guide others toward the blessing of new life through Christ and continued transformation through His Spirit.

NOTES

....

....

....

....

....

....

....

....

....

....

....

....

....

....

....

....

....

....

....

....

....

....

....

DISCIPLES PATH
Group Directory

Name: _____

Home Phone: _____

Mobile Phone: _____

Email: _____

Social Media: _____

Name: _____

Home Phone: _____

Mobile Phone: _____

Email: _____

Social Media: _____

Name: _____

Home Phone: _____

Mobile Phone: _____

Email: _____

Social Media: _____

Name: _____

Home Phone: _____

Mobile Phone: _____

Email: _____

Social Media: _____

Name: _____

Home Phone: _____

Mobile Phone: _____

Email: _____

Social Media: _____

Name: _____

Home Phone: _____

Mobile Phone: _____

Email: _____

Social Media: _____

Name: _____

Home Phone: _____

Mobile Phone: _____

Email: _____

Social Media: _____

Name: _____

Home Phone: _____

Mobile Phone: _____

Email: _____

Social Media: _____

Name: _____

Home Phone: _____

Mobile Phone: _____

Email: _____

Social Media: _____

Name: _____

Home Phone: _____

Mobile Phone: _____

Email: _____

Social Media: _____